The Transformation of Dogma

An Introduction to Karl Rahner on Doctrine

Mary E. Hines

PAULIST PRESS  New York/Mahwah

ACKNOWLEDGEMENTS

Excerpts from the following were used with permission: *Foundations of Christian Faith* by Karl Rahner; *Theological Investigations*, Vols. IV, XIV, XVI; *Faith in History and Society* by Johann Baptist Metz; *Kerygma and Dogma* by Karl Rahner—all published by Crossroad/Continuum, New York, N.Y.

Library of Congress Cataloging-in-Publication Data

Hines, Mary E., 1943–
    The transformation of dogma: an introduction to Karl Rahner on doctrine / Mary E. Hines.
      p. cm.
    Includes bibliographies.
    ISBN 0-8091-3072-6: $6.95 (est.)
    1. Rahner, Karl. 1904-   . 2. Catholic Church—Doctrines-History —20th century. 3. Theology, Doctrinal—History—20th century. 4. Dogma—History—20th century. I. Title.
    BX4705.R287H56   1989
    230'.2'0924——dc19   89-31094
                                                            CIP

Published by Paulist Press
997 Macarthur Boulevard
Mahwah, NJ 07430

Printed and bound in the
United States of America

Contents

Introduction

What do the dogmas and doctrines of the church have to do with the challenge of living Christian life today? Must we believe in all the various dogmas that the church has accumulated over its long history, many of which seem far removed from the compelling issues of life today—the threat of nuclear war, ecological destruction of the planet, discrimination based on race or sex, human hunger—to name but a few? How does dogma relate to other formulations of faith such as scripture, creeds, theological statements and other magisterial statements? How should the church's teaching office exercise its role today and in the future? Is dogma still necessary in today's church and world or is it an obstacle to getting in touch with the mystery that lies at the heart of religious faith, personal experience of the living God? Do the dogmas distract from the praxiological concerns of today's political and liberation theologies? These are only some of the questions addressed to the issue of dogma today. They are at the root of contemporary controversies over the Catholic's right to dissent from church dogma and from authentic non-infallible teaching.

Karl Rahner, acknowledged as a theological giant of the twentieth century, reflected on these questions frequently over the course of his long theological career. In fact the question of dogma is so central to Rahner's theology that a focus on this issue provides not only an introduction to the problem of dogma but also a good entry into Rahner's whole theological endeavor. His own thought developed and changed along with the changing church of the volatile period in which he lived and wrote.

Although Rahner's writings on dogma provide no easy answers to today's controversies, they do provide a beginning point and a framework sensitive both to the church's tradition and to today's needs. He deals with the root questions of dogma so fundamental to developing responsible positions concerning the specific problems of today.

Although dogma is a particular problem for Catholic Christians, Rahner's work has a wider significance because he always situates his discussion of dogma within the whole context of the nature, development and legitimacy of formulations of faith in general. He focuses especially on those formulations which have attained authoritative status through their centrality to the Christian mystery and their long history of acceptance by the church community. A significant problem today is that even these central truths of faith have become detached not only from our own experience but from the original experience of faith out of which they arose, experience of the self-revealing God whose human face is revealed to us in the life, death and resurrection of Jesus Christ. Presented this way, the doctrines of faith can seem alien propositions requiring external obedience but foreign to our lives. Rahner aims to restore the link between doctrine and experience. He calls for a hermeneutics of doctrine that reinterprets and reunderstands the central doctrines within our new historical horizon, in our language and thought frameworks, with our questions. In his later writings he goes beyond this to envision the future functioning of faith formulations in the world-church which has been inaugurated by Vatican II in a way very different from the past. In this vision, a plurality and diversity of faith formulations arising out of local churches could facilitate our entry into a mystical contemplation of the central realities of faith which would undergird and motivate our action to address the compelling issues of our world.

CHAPTER 1

Dogma and Experience

Earlier in this century the Roman Catholic modernists[1] wrestled with the issue of dogma. They rebelled against the authoritarian imposition of dogma by the magisterium and against the identification of faith with the acceptance of certain propositions. They saw dogma as essentially timebound and changeable. Religious truth, they said, is grounded in human experience of the divine. Propositions of faith bear no intrinsic connection to the reality they attempt to articulate. The modernists denied that any statement could belong to the constitution of religious experience itself. Therefore they could only see dogma as secondary and derivative with regard to the experience it attempts to articulate. Experience itself is the only valid way to get in touch with religious reality, and conceptual reflection is always a step away from that experience and a purely human reflection on it.

Rahner's Theological Anthropology

Karl Rahner's theological anthropology offers a basis for accepting the fundamental insight of the modernists, that faith must grow out of actual human experience, as well as a grounding for a more positive assessment of the possibility of conceptual formulations which articulate that experience. In an effort to understand the human person in his or her relation to God he presents a nuanced understanding of experience and its relation to articulation which attempts to avoid the immanentism[2] of which the modernists were accused. He also avoids the extrinsicism typified by the anti-modernist reaction which, in an extreme form in *Lamentabili sane Exitu*, the 1907 decree condemning a number of propositions which it attributed to "modernism," condemned the view that dogmas had not fallen fully developed from heaven.

In Rahner's view there is no fundamental opposition between an experientially grounded understanding of religion and an understanding which gives a central importance to formulations of faith. His approach to human knowing and being offers a way to overcome the dichotomy, which the modernists and others were unable to bridge, between that experience which is foundational to all religious faith and the propositional formulation of that experience.

This chapter views dogma in a wider sense than that which has become customary since the eighteenth century.[3] It does not yet distinguish the various modes of the articulation of revelation, i.e., scripture, theology, dogma. A more precise delimitation of dogma from other types of religious and secular statements will follow in later chapters. The focus here is on the problem foundational to all these modes of expression, which is the relationship of conceptualization to the original experience which it attempts to articulate. In other words, can there be a statement of an experienced reality which is so close to the reality that it can in fact bring us into touch with that reality, rather than leading away from it?

To get at this foundational issue the meaning of experience must be explored more fully. Rahner's approach enables him to agree with the modernist notion that dogma does arise out of human self-experience, but he accounts for this in a more nuanced way so that, for him, human experience is never *merely* human. By grounding dogma in a conceptualizing moment at the heart of human self-experience, Rahner opens a way to save dogma from the critique of those who view it as purely extrinsic and secondary.

The Meaning of Experience

Dermot Lane offers a clear preliminary description of experience as this chapter will use it. "Experience . . . is the product that arises out of the interaction that takes place between the subject and reality." He goes on to relate experience in general with religious experience. "Ordinary experiences may be described as those everyday subject-object encounters we have in life. . . . [In religious experience] a disclosure is made through the medium of a human experience. This disclosure is identified with what is called the religious dimension of life."[4] Lane refers to what Rahner calls transcendental experience as the depth dimension present in all human experience. Much of this chapter will be devoted to further exploration of Rahner's understanding of the meaning of this fundamental depth experience and its relationship to conceptualization.

The starting point for Rahner's anthropology reflects the philosophical turn to the subject prevalent since Kant and the Enlightenment. Human beings are able to experience themselves as subjects and as persons.[5] They are able to raise questions about themselves. The content of this experience of oneself as person and subject is first of all, and most generally, a recognition of limitation. The person recognizes himself or herself as not infinite but as finite, as not self-produced but as essentially *thrown* into the world. Thus one experiences oneself as questioner — as looking out beyond oneself for the answer to the question of existence.

This ability to be present to oneself, to ask questions about oneself, is the distinguishing characteristic of *human* being. Self-presence is thus the most fundamental act of human knowledge for Rahner. Primary in knowledge is not a knowledge of a variety of objects outside the self (although he is clear that knowledge does not consist in innate ideas but comes through the senses), but the self-awareness or self-presence we experience *in* the act of knowing persons and things in the world. This self-presence or experience of the self as subject always involves the human being's unthematic or unreflexive awareness of an infinite horizon present in every act of knowlege. In other words, the experience of self and of objects as limited, as not the totality of being, presumes the unthematic, or as yet vague and unarticulated, awareness of limitless being or of the totality of being. In the act of knowing, human beings experience themselves as drawn beyond themselves toward this ultimate horizon of being. This is what Rahner means by transcendence.

For Rahner, life's deepest mystery is that this horizon, the totality of being, has chosen freely to reveal itself to men and women as God — the goal of their transcendence. Thus in every act of knowing the human being experiences, as well as the external reality, both himself or herself and God the horizon of all being. The experience of self and of God, co-present in all acts of knowing according to Rahner, is the essential foundation for all further reflection. This is transcendental experience, the original non-thematic consciousness of the transcendent self which is present in every act of human knowing. This fundamental experience is the foundation for all further reflexive knowledge, but is prior to it.[6] Through God's gracious self-revelation the "whither" of this human experience of transcendence can be recognized as God. For Rahner, it is clear that faith arises in the first instance in this original experience rather than in confrontation with propositions. By emphasizing the unity of experience of self and of God Rahner brings an important dimension to the statement attributed to the modernists that concepts arise out of the human being's experience of self. In his understanding, this immediately implies that they arise out of his or her experience of God at the same time. How does Rahner account for this fundamental unity of our experience of self and of God?

The Fundamental Unity of the Experience of God and of Self

Rahner refers to the co-experience of self and God as original experience which is common to all people. It is foundational to all particular experiences. He emphasizes that the experience of God involved in this unity may well be unexplicitated or un-thematic. In other words, even those share in this experience who would not use the word God or consciously advert to God's presence. In every act of knowledge the external reality to be known constitutes the *a posteriori* content of knowledge, and the experience of God and the self constitutes its *a priori* or transcendental aspect. This experience of God and of self exists in a fundamental unity; they co-determine each other.[7] "This unity consists far more in the fact that the original and ultimate experience of *God* constitutes the enabling condition of, and an intrinsic element in, the experience of self in such a way that without this experience of God no experience of self is possible."[8]

For this reason, Rahner goes on to state, "the personal history of experience of the self is the personal history of the experience of God."[9] Whatever reflexive articulation grows out of one's experience of self grows out of and is determined at the same time by one's experience of God. In this way Rahner avoids the immanentism of which the modernists were accused when he says that this original experience out of which all explication grows is prior to any conceptualization or reflection. He has united immanence and transcendence right at the initial point out of which all statements about what he calls the "holy mystery" originate.

By describing God as the ultimate horizon of all human knowledge Rahner avoids misunderstanding God as an object among other objects of human knowledge as God has often been portrayed through history. To underline this he often avoids the word God. "Since we mean God as he is implicitly known in everything...and not as he is explicitly known and subsequently described, we cannot simply say God."[10] Rahner suggests that more appropriate designations for this reality might be "the nameless, that which is other than all finite things, the infinite,"[11] or, as he so often prefers himself, "the holy mystery."

In summary then, when Rahner refers to transcendental experience, he means that unthematic awareness of self and of God which is co-present in every act of knowing. Although this experience is present unexplicitly in all of our everyday activity, it imposes itself upon us in a more intense way in certain "limit" experiences which cause us to come face to face with certain realities which we generally might not advert to. Rahner cites aloneness, responsibility, love and death as instances of such moments.[12] We sometimes call these graced moments because they are particularly disclosive of the always present free offer of God's self gift, although in Rahner's view *all* our moments are graced.

Experience as Graced Experience

Rahner's work on grace is central to his theology and is necessary to a fuller understanding of the unity of the experience of self and God. To the question of whether this experience of self and of God belongs to the order of nature or of grace, Rahner replies, "We would have to describe this experience in the concrete situation of our human lives as belonging both to 'nature' *and* to 'grace' at the same time."[13] Since human beings always stand under the offer of grace all of their activity is transformed by this dimension of their experience. "Human transcendence, ordered to God in freedom and knowledge, is always and inescapably deepened, whether this is accepted or rejected, by what in Christian terms is called grace."[14] When human beings experience God not merely as the hidden and distant goal of their transcendence, but rather as near and accessible, although remaining mystery, grace can be said to be operative.

Rahner is opposed to a common understanding of grace, prevalent in the last few centuries, which saw it essentially as a commodity added to the human being's already constituted nature — a sort of supernatural second story added to an already complete natural one. In this understanding grace is purely external, outside human consciousness or experience, so whatever human beings come to know by reflecting on their own experience would be "pure nature." This led subscribers to this view to develop an anthropology in which pure nature could be clearly distinguished from the supernatural in humankind.

To say within this framework that dogma arises out of human experience, as did the modernists, would be understood to make dogma a conceptual development of the person's purely natural experience. Obviously experience understood this way would be a problematic start for any kind of theological reflection. In opposition to this, adherents of the two story anthropology insisted that theological reflection should more properly start from that verbal revelation from without, i.e., scripture and tradition, which is the human being's only avenue of contact with the supernatural. Dogma would be an element of the supernatural second story, superimposed but not intrinsic to human experience. Within this framework then dogma is either a merely human phenomenon arising from experience, or entirely divine, divorced from human experience.

Rahner offers a way out of this impasse. In opposition to

the reified notion of grace operative in the view described above, he sees grace as the personal self-communication of God to the individual. This communication is not a word about God, but the very reality of God's own self which informs and transforms the human being. It does not arbitrarily impinge as a foreign element on a fully constituted human nature, because the possibility of the human being's reception of this self-communication of God is predicated on his or her transcendental constitution as oriented, toward the incomprehensible mystery as goal and term. Because of the transcendental openness of the human constitution, when the holy mystery graciously and freely chooses to draw near to human beings, they are able to grasp freely and to experience this mystery as the true fulfillment of their transcendental longing. Rahner thus avoids the extrinsicism of the two-story theory.

This movement of grace or self-communication of God is not a sporadic event in the lives of men and women. It is not subject to individual merit, and it exists prior to human sin although human freedom allows for the possible rejection of God's self-offer. Thus Rahner says that this gratuitous offer of God's grace is a permanent existential in the lives of human beings — a ''supernatural existential.'' So *de facto* grace, which is the self-communication of God, lies at the very heart of human existence co-determining all human action and reflection. ''In the one and only concrete, real order of human existence, what is most intrinsic to man is God's self-communication at least as an offer, and as given prior to man's freedom as the condition of its highest and obligatory actualization.''[15] It is clear then that, for Rahner, the fundamental experience lying at the heart of human existence arises out of the human being's always and already graced nature. To say that dogma must be intrinsically connected to *human* experience does not challenge its graced reality.

To safeguard the freedom of God and avoid any suggestion that grace is a necessity, violating either God's freedom or human freedom, Rahner holds onto the idea of pure nature as a remainder concept. Theoretically if one subtracted the supernatural existential from human existence, one would have pure nature. In the concrete order of existence, however, there is no real line between nature and supernature because *de facto* from the first moment of existence the human being has been constituted by the free offer of God's grace. Because nature and grace are so deeply intertwined at the core of human existence, "our actual nature is *never* 'pure' nature. . . . It is a nature which is continually being determined (which does not mean justified) by the supernatural grace of salvation offered to it."[16]

Most importantly according to Rahner this grace is *consciously* experienced. Thus when we experience ourselves in the fundamental human experience of transcendence we never in fact experience pure nature, but we experience ourselves always as graced. We may not experience grace *as* grace, i.e., reflexively as an object, but we do experience grace.

Verbal revelation helps in interpreting one's experience unambiguously and with reflexive certainty, but even those who have no contact with historical Christianity consciously, if unreflexively, experience grace. Where and how do we experience grace? Grace is felt in the deepest experiences of humankind, "the experience of infinite longings, of radical optimism, of unquenchable discontent, of the torment of the insufficiency of everything attainable, of the radical protest against death, the experience of being confronted with an absolute love precisely where it is lethally incomprehensible and seems to be silent and aloof, the experience of a radical guilt and of a still abiding hope etc."[17] In all these human experiences, Rahner says, human beings experience not merely their human nature — but both grace and nature. It is through these "limit" experiences that the transcendental experience of grace present in all human activity can most easily come to reflexive awareness.

To summarize then: Since human beings always experience themselves as oriented toward the absolute, and since this absolute has revealed itself as gracious and accessible to human existence, then human experience is always at the same time experience of the self-communicating God — it is always graced experience. The key question for dogma is how the articulation of this fundamental experience is related to the experience itself.

The Relationship of Experience and Concept

To describe this relationship, Rahner uses an analogy to the situation of a young person who is taken up in the experience of a deep love. "This love may have *presuppositions* (of a metaphysical, psychological and physiological kind) which are simply unknown to him. His love *itself* is his 'experience'; he is conscious of it, lives through it with the entire fullness and depth of a real love."[18]

Following along with this analogy Rahner asks what role is played by the attempt at conceptualization of this experience of love. Do concepts necessarily distort and draw one away from the reality which they attempt to express? Can there be a statement, such as dogma, which claims to be a true and lasting articulation of the reality to which it refers? If original experience is truly experience of God and of self, is the attempt to describe it always a *merely* human word? According to Rahner, the reflexive moment, the move toward conceptualization, may be secondary but it is intimately tied to original experience. When the lover experiences love he or she is always led to reflect on this experience and to attempt to articulate it in whatever way possible — inadequate though it may be. And the love itself grows and is deepened by its expression. On the same analogy, original experience strains toward articulation which in turn deepens and clarifies that experience. "Original, non-propositional, unreflexive yet conscious possession of a reality on the one hand, and reflexive (propositional), articulated consciousness of this original consciousness on the other — these are not competing opposites but reciprocally interacting factors of a single experience necessarily unfolding in historical succession."[19]

The philosophical grounding for this very basic under-pinning of Rahner's understanding of dogma is found in his epistemology, or metaphysics of knowledge.[20] Three aspects of this metaphysics of knowledge are particularly significant for a discussion of dogma: his affirmation of the original unity of being and knowing, his notion of the pre apprehension of being as the condition of the possibility for all *a posteriori* knowing, and his discussion of the conceptual moment as a secondary but intrinsic element in the act of knowing.

Rahner's understanding of the act of knowing must be briefly sketched to see how all these elements fit into the whole. This is developed in his early philosophical work, *Spirit in the World,* which is an attempt to relate the epistemology of Thomas Aquinas to the insights of modern philosophy, particularly Kant.[21]

Spirit in the World takes as its starting point the human being as questioner. Discovering himself or herself situated in the world, the human being asks the question about his or her existence. Rahner asserts that the very asking of the question about being affirms a sort of pre-knowledge about the totality of being. In the face of a vague knowledge of the totality, human beings recognize themselves as limited or finite — not the totality of being. Thus in this original experience of the human being as questioner there is also revealed a knowledge in the knower which is a presence to self. According to Rahner this presence to self is the primordial aspect of knowing and is in fact the very being of the knower. He asserts that the intensity of being in a being is in proportion to its knowability in this primordial sense of presence to self, thus the unity of being and knowing.

Out of this conviction about the fundamental unity of being and knowing Rahner develops the metaphysics of knowledge which lays the groundwork for all his later theological efforts. His understanding of dogma and its development grows out of this understanding of human being and knowing. A short and simplified account of this material follows, highlighting those aspects important to an understanding of dogma.[22] According to Rahner, following Thomas, all human knowing takes place through the senses. One does not know from innate ideas, or through an abstract relating of concepts. One knows only in relationship to reality. But at the same time the knowledge of outside reality is never just received into the intellect as an image or copy.[23]

In the act of knowledge, as Rahner understands it, the knower knows both the reality to be apprehended and himself or herself. ''In knowledge not only is something known, but the subject's knowing is always co-known.''[24] This presence to self is conscious but as yet unthematic, that is, not made an object of explicit reflection. Rahner calls the presence to self, that is part of the structure of every act of knowledge, transcendental experience, or ''the subjective, unthematic necessary and unfailing consciousness of the knowing subject that is co-present in every spiritual act of knowledge, and the subject's openness to the unlimited expanse of all possible reality.''[25] This is a more philosophical description of that fundamental experience of self described above.

The second part of this definition refers to what Rahner calls the pre-apprehension of being. In every act of knowledge, not only is there an experience of self-presence and an apprehension of the particular reality to be known but this takes place in the context of a vague grasp of the totality of all being which allows the recognition of particular beings. This pre-apprehension is the condition of the possibility of any objective knowledge. This pre-apprehension is not to be understood as an object among other objects of knowledge. "The pre-apprehension (and its 'whither') is known insofar as knowledge, in the apprehension of its individual object, always experiences itself as already and always moving out beyond it, insofar as it knows the object in the horizon of its possible objects in such a way that the pre-apprehension reveals itself in the movement out towards the totality of the objects."[26]

Although not objectified, nevertheless the pre-apprehension is real because *esse* always means for Thomas (and for Rahner) to be real. It can never be merely a principle of understanding — a formal principle.[27] Thus, for Thomas, "to-be-in-itself *(Ansichsein)* and *esse* or to-be-real *(Wirklichsein)* coincide. . . . Objective knowing attains to real being in principle."[28] This means that for Thomas (and for Rahner) truth is located in this fact — that the intellect attains to the being of things. The truth of propositions then is never eternal universal truth but the "truth of the intellect attaining to the in-itself of real being."[29] This understanding of the truth of propositions as growing out of the fundamental experience of human being and knowing which can attain to the reality of being in itself is a significant factor in Rahner's understanding of the truth claim of propositions in general and more specifically in the case of dogma.

A second and related point with regard to the pre-apprehension of being as an unthematic grasp of the totality of all being is Rahner's use of this concept as the starting point for his theory of the development of dogma. Instead of the understanding, common at this time, which saw dogma developing in logical progression from original propositions, Rahner suggests that we consider dogma as developing out of this original unthematic grasp of the totality. I have already referred above to Rahner's use of the experience of love which is only gradually and stumblingly articulated. Rahner expresses the idea more theoretically as follows: "It is not (merely) a matter of the logical development and inference of new propositions from earlier ones, but of the formulation for the first time of propositions about a knowledge already possessed, in an infinite search which only approaches its goal asymptotically."[30] Rahner applies this insight from his early philosophy to his developing theological thought on dogma. Dogma may be understood to develop out of an original unthematic grasp of the whole of revelation rather than in a linear or logical progression from an original set of propositions as the "deposit of faith" theology prevalent at the time implied. This will be developed further in the following chapter on revelation and dogma.

The final point to be considered in relation to Rahner's metaphysics of knowledge is the problem raised at the beginning regarding the relationship of original experience to its conceptualization. Rahner specifically locates his discussion of this issue in the context of the poles of, on the one hand, rationalism, which understood knowledge as occurring through concepts, and, on the other, classical modernism, which was understood to locate it exclusively in experience and which regarded conceptualization as very secondary.

> Basically every rationalism is based upon the conviction that a reality is present for man in spiritual and free self-possession only through the objectifying concept, and this becomes genuinely and fully real in scientific knowledge. Conversely, what is called 'modernism' in the classical understanding lives by the conviction that the concept or reflection is something *absolutely* secondary in relation to the original self-possession of existence in self-consciousness and freedom, so that reflection could also be dispensed with.[31]

Rahner wants to find a middle way. He is convinced that experience is primary, but at the same time he holds to the value and necessity of bringing that experience to expression in concepts and propositions. In fact he says that conceptualization is integral to experience. "There is in man an inescapable *unity in difference between one's original self-possession and reflection.*" [32] Conceptualization may be a second moment but it does belong to the original knowledge and in fact the tendency toward conceptualization is part of the inner dynamism of the act of knowledge. Rahner goes so far as to say, "At that moment when this element of reflection would no longer be present, this original self-possession would also cease to exist."[33]

For Rahner, then, conceptualization is not a negative perversion of the original experience but rather an integral part of it. "We could show again and again that all these theological concepts do not make the reality itself present to man from outside of him, but they are rather the expression of what has already been experienced and lived through more originally in the depths of existence."[34] He also asserts strongly that no attempt at conceptualization ever captures completely the original experience. "But this conceptualized and thematized self-presence of the subject and its knowing is never identical with the original self-presence and never recaptures its content completely."[35]

Most important, for Rahner, is that though experience is primary, the concept is in real touch with that experience and expresses it truly if always inadequately. In fact, he says that since all reflection takes place in orientation to the original experience, it in addition to its development outward, always also leads back into the original unity of being.[36] This dynamism in the act of knowing as a move toward conceptualization on the one hand, with a corresponding return to the unity of the original experience on the other, is a paradigm for Rahner's understanding of the dynamism of dogmatic development — a paradigm which he emphasizes more and more in his developing reflections on dogma.

The idea of dogma, seen as growing out of the moment of conceptualization inherent in the act of knowing, is, therefore, not foreign to human experience but rather follows from the very nature of human being and knowing. On the other hand, however, Rahner stresses that concomitant with the need for the development of original experience into ever increasing conceptualizations, which refine and make its meaning explicit, is an equally strong impetus to return to the simplicity and unity of the original experience.

Although Rahner defends the legitimacy and necessity of dogmatic development with its increasing clarification and differentiation as it has taken place in the context of the evolving self-understanding of the church, his natural inclination seems to be more toward contemplation of the incomprehensible mystery, as he calls God, as it is experienced in its simplicity and unity in transcendental experience. ''The most primordial, underivative knowledge of God, which is the basis of all other knowledge of God, is given in the experience of transcendence, insofar as it contains, implicitly and unobjectivated, but irrecusably and inevitably the 'Whither' of transcendence, which we call God.''[37] Thus, there appears to be in fact if not in theory a certain relativization of formulations which becomes more overt as his theology develops.

This discussion of the relationship of experience and concept is fundamental to any understanding of Rahner's approach to dogma. It obviously leaves certain unresolved ambiguities. In spite of his theoretical insistence on the permanent significance of past formulations and the need for present experience to find its way to expression, does Rahner's inclination toward the transcendental not in fact relativize the significance for faith of conceptual formulations? This issue will come up again in following chapters.

Symbol as the Expression of Being

One further area which provides significant background for Rahner's understanding of dogma is his theology of symbol and his understanding of the symbolic nature of word. According to Rahner, being is essentially expressive, that is, it must go out of itself in order to be itself. The possibility of self-experience and experience of God which was discussed above is grounded in the fact that being is of its very nature symbolic or expressive. "A being comes to itself by means of 'expression', insofar as it comes to itself at all. The expression, that is, the 'symbol' . . . is the way of knowledge of self, possession of self, in general."[38] The deepest and most intense meaning of symbol is that expression which constitutes a plurality at the heart of being itself and which is encompassed within the original unity. It is through expression that being comes to that self-possession which is characteristic to a greater or lesser degree of both human and divine being.

The symbol is that by which the reality communicates itself *ad extra*. So the dynamism which lies at the heart of being, the dynamism which leads to self-experience, is also a dynamism which leads to expression *ad extra*. Being is thus essentially expressive. The mode of its presenting itself for knowledge by another can be known as "symbol." This is a mode of presentation which does not present an arbitrary representation of itself — but brings another into contact with the reality itself. Clearly, for Rahner, symbol is a very strong concept.

Rahner explains this understanding of symbol more clearly by relating it to his understanding of Trinity. The immanent relations within the Trinity ground the activity of the economic Trinity. "It is because God 'must' 'express' himself inwardly that he can also utter himself outwardly; the finite, created utterance *ad extra* is a continuation of the immanent constitution of 'image and likeness.' "[39] This utterance *ad extra* is the Logos, the incarnate Word, "the absolute symbol of God in the world."[40] The symbol, therefore, is the expression of that which is being symbolized, rendering it present to another or others.

The theory of symbol underlines Rahner's belief that the expression of that inner experience that lies at the heart of being is not absolutely secondary and derivative leading away from the reality but in fact can be the real means of access to that reality. A very concrete means of understanding this conception is Rahner's conviction that the human body is symbolic of the human person. It is through the body that human beings express themselves to the world and it is through the body that others encounter the whole person.

Rahner applies this powerful notion of symbol to his understanding of church as the continuing presence in time of the Logos, and to the sacraments as the concrete actualizations of that continuing symbolic presence of Christ in space and time which is the church. It is not difficult to see how this same understanding of symbolic reality could underpin his understanding of the dogmas as words of the church in its ongoing historical existence. Dogma as part of the realization of the church in different times and circumstances can be seen as participating in the symbolic reality that is the church — and, therefore, as bringing us into real touch with that mystery which is brought to expression in it.

Of particular interest to a discussion of dogma is Rahner's discussion of the symbolic efficacy of word. He offers the possibility of understanding sacraments as subordinate to a wider notion of *word* as *the* effective symbol of God in the world and, therefore, as the primary symbol by which the church actualizes itself in the world. This underlines once again Rahner's conviction that the bringing to expression of original experience is a constitutive element of that experience — an element that is in touch with and makes present that original reality rather than leading away from it. All the affirmations made about symbolic reality hold true, in the deepest sense, of word. Rahner makes this clear in a note to the article, "What Is a Sacrament?"

> The word of God in its full and original sense is not to be conceived of as belonging to the level of instruction in propositional form 'about something', nor merely as pointing in an intentional sense to a state of affairs which for its part is totally independent of this instructional reference. Rather it is to be conceived of as an exhibitive word, a word that renders present. It is in it and through it that the reality designated is first and foremost given, and, moreover, in a relationship of mutual conditioning of such a kind that the word is constituted by the reality which thereby comes to be, and the reality comes to be in that, and because, it reveals itself in this way.[41]

According to Rahner, all words spoken by and in the church participate in a more or less intense fashion in this primordial event character of the word of God. Words such as catechetical information, which are a step removed from the reality which they describe, "have the function of preparing for, surrounding, or following from this true word, the exhibitive word of grace, and are oriented to it."[42] Rahner explicitly puts the word of dogma within the context of the inherently symbolic or sacramental nature (recalling his understanding of symbolic reality) of word. "Dogma is not merely a statement 'about' something, but one in which, because it is an 'exhibitive' word with a 'sacramental' nature, what it states actually occurs and is posited by its existence: God's self-communication in grace which is also the grace of its absolute acceptance (faith)."[43]

Rahner's focus on the importance of "word" as the primary symbol which makes present the mystery of God in the world brings us to the final issue of this chapter — a preliminary discussion of Rahner's understanding of revelation, a discussion which will be developed more concretely in Chapter 2.

Revelation and Word

Since revelation in Rahner usually means God's self-communication to humankind and the unfolding of this self-communication in history, it is obviously of foundational significance for his treatment of dogma. Grace, understood as God's self-communication to humankind, is the primordial meaning of revelation or what Rahner refers to as transcendental revelation. The question is: *How* does the transcendental experience of God present in every act of knowledge enter into history? Chapter 2 will discuss further the concrete history of revelation but it is first necessary to consider the philosophical background for his understanding of revelation, especially as this is contained in *Hearers of the Word*.

This second of Rahner's early philosophical works tries to lay bare the anthropological presuppositions for the possible hearing of revelation. This understanding of revelation lays the groundwork for Rahner's explanation of how God's word is received through history by women and men, and is the context in which dogma must be situated.[44] Rahner's theological interpretation of revelation rests again on his philosophical anthropology. He sees human persons as intrinsically oriented toward the absolute — toward the horizon of their existence —

toward the totality of being. The experience of limitedness which is the human being's reaction to his or her awareness of unlimited being leads the human being to experience himself or herself as question and therefore as one who is on the lookout for an answer to this question, the question of one's own existence. The central mystery of Christianity for Rahner is that human beings are not doomed to remain eternally frustrated — their constitutive transcendence reaching out to a distant, silent and aloof horizon — but that this horizon has freely chosen not to remain distant but to draw near. This, for Rahner, is the fundamental meaning of revelation, the gratuitous self-communication of God to human beings, a communication which they are able to hear and accept because of the fundamental openness of their human constitution. Human beings, then, do not experience God's revelation as exterior or foreign but as the answer to the question that is human existence.

Thus far this description of revelation echoes the explanation of grace outlined above, but for a complete understanding of revelation two new elements need to be emphasized. The first is that although the transcendental aspect of revelation is fundamental to Rahner's understanding, it must never be forgotten that revelation is *always* mediated historically. This Rahner refers to as categorical revelation. "The revelation event itself, therefore, always has two sides. On the one hand it constitutes man's supernaturally elevated transcendence as his permanent though grace-given destiny. . . . On the other hand, the revelation event is also the historical mediation, the objective, explicit expression of the supernaturally transcendental experience. It occurs in history."[45] The fact that transcendental and categorical revelation constitute two aspects of the *one* revelation, in Rahner's understanding, echoes his philosophical conviction about the relationship of experience and concept. The transcendental experience of God's self-communication bears within itself the dynamism to become thematic and explicit and this explicitation is able, in fact, to bring us into touch with that original experience rather than leading us away from it.

The second element to be emphasized more explicitly is that revelation as dialogic event encompasses within itself both God's communication and human hearing and response. This is most graphically demonstrated in the climax of revelation, the event of Jesus Christ in whom is revealed "the absolute and irrevocable unity of God's transcendental self-communication to mankind and of its historical mediation . . . at once God himself as communicated, the human acceptance of this communication and the final historical manifestation of this offer and acceptance."[46] Because of this unity of the transcendental and categorical, God's revelation enters into history in human words as the essential, but always limited, attempt to verbalize the original experience of revelation. The ongoing human attempt to express the experience of God's self-communication, Rahner refers to as the history of revelation.

Since revelation and its conceptualization share the basic structure of the act of knowledge, statements which attempt to communicate the reality of God show both the tendency to move out and become more explicit and rational, and at the same time, since all such statements are formed in vital contact with the living reality of God's self, they show a corresponding tendency to return to the original unity which they attempt to describe in a limited way. Thus the interpretative human word can, under certain circumstances, be seen as a constitutive element of revelation — not just a word about revelation but actually the word of God itself.

"Word" for Rahner does not only or in the first instance mean an external phonetic symbol which impinges upon the human being from the outside. This is the second stage. Prior to that, at least logically, "word" is intrinsic to the transcendental experience of revelation. "And that grace-given fundamental subjective attitude of man, which is directed towards the God of triune life, can quite definitely be regarded as a word-revelation, provided the notion of word is not reduced to that of a phonetic utterance.''[47] Word, then, is not secondary to the transcendental experience of revelation but lies at its very heart. Rahner reminds us that transcendental revelation is always historically mediated even in this original experience which always involves contact with historical reality. God's revelation passes into history in human words whose ability to make present the reality which they articulate grows out of the fundamental presence of word, which is at the heart of the original revelation experience.

This discussion of the philosophical presuppositions for the possibility of revelation points out that for Rahner the original experience of revelation includes within it the subjective response of human beings as intrinsic to it and that this response may properly be called ''word.'' This may be seen as grounding the reality and truth of attempts at conceptualization of this experience *ad extra* in much the same fashion as does Rahner's understanding of the relations of the immanent and economic Trinity. Immanent activity bears within itself the dynamism to become explicit, but the explicitation is only possible because of the immanent activity.

Rahner's anthropology as outlined in *Hearers of the Word*, which focuses particularly on the historical constitution of human beings, lays the groundwork for a possible understanding of the importance of human formulations of revelation since it sees that human activity is at the very core of the revelation event. ''In whatever way revelation may originally take place, it has to be transposed into the human word, if man is not to be taken by revelation out of his human way of existing.''[48]

The focus in this chapter has been on the role of experience in Rahner's work and its relationship to conceptualization. It has defined experience, as Rahner understands it, both philosophically and theologically. Both Rahner's metaphysics of knowledge and his understanding of revelation, which grows out of this, support the view that Rahner sees experience, as defined above, as the primary and fundamental meaning of knowledge and as the beginning of faith. We know, not first from external propositions, but from our experience of self which is at the same time experience of God. It is out of this experience that reflection grows.

But in contrast to immanentism, Rahner holds that self-experience is never *merely* human experience but always also the experience of God. He also holds that the moment of reflection is not *absolutely* secondary and derivative but in fact belongs to the constitution of experience as a secondary but essential moment. This understanding is borne out by his works on word and symbol and by his writings on revelation which always see it as *one* event involving God's action and human response. It is clear from the above that for Rahner, to affirm experience as the starting point for theology in no way implies the necessity of abandoning the propositional. His grounding of conceptualization at the very heart of original human experience and his strong theology of symbol allow Rahner to be able to affirm both experience *and* propositional formulations of that experience, such as dogma, as fundamental to religion.

Notes

¹ Although "modernist" was a label applied to a disparate group of people with disparate theological views, these views were often collapsed together to describe a position called "modernist." I rely here on Rahner's understanding of modernism which he uses as a dialectical tool against which to differentiate his own positions on dogma. See Rahner, "Dogma," *Encyclopedia of Theology: The Concise Sacramentum Mundi,* ed. Karl Rahner (New York: Seabury Press, 1975), 355-356. The *Encyclopedia of Theology* is hereafter cited as *ET.* For a more complete discussion of the complex phenomenon of modernism see Aubert, "Modernism," *ET:* 969-974.

² *ET* defines immanentism as follows: "Immanentism is the name given to the doctrine or attitude which excludes transcendence, that is, the reference to 'the other' in any form whatever, on the grounds that the other is to be found equivalently in the subject itself." This was the immanentism of which the modernists were accused (whether rightly or wrongly) and which was condemned by the church. There is, however, a Christian understanding of immanence which, while recognizing that "all knowing involves inner self-realization," recognizes also the reality of a transcendental dimension of existence. Peter Henrici, "Immanentism," *ET:* 686-687. Rahner differentiates himself from the approach condemned by the church and attempts in his theology to unite the immanent and transcendent dimensions of experience. For further and more in depth treatment of the understanding of immanence in the modernist period and in post-modernist Catholic theology, see Gregory Baum, *Man Becoming* (New York: Seabury, 1970) and Gabriel Daly, *Transcendence and Immanence: A Study in Catholic Modernism and Integralism* (Oxford: Clarendon Press, 1980).

³ Karl Rahner and Karl Lehmann, *Kerygma and Dogma* (New York: Herder and Herder, 1969), p. 34.

⁴ Dermot Lane, *The Experience of God: An Invitation To Do Theology* (New York: Paulist Press, 1981), pp. 9 and 12-13.

⁵ Karl Rahner, *Foundations of Christian Faith,* trans. William V. Dych (New York: Seabury, 1978), pp. 28, 29.

⁶ Karl Rahner, "Experience of Self and Experience of God," *Theological Investigations* XIII, trans. David Bourke (New York: Seabury, 1975), pp. 124-125. Further references to *Theological Investigations* will be cited as *TI* and Rahner's name will be omitted.

⁷ See James Bacik, *Apologetics and the Eclipse of Mystery* (Notre Dame: Univ. of Notre Dame Press, 1980), pp. 27-36, for his discussion of the relationship between the experience of God and self-experience. He cautions against any absolute identity of self and God such as would lead to pantheism. Rahner's careful insistence on the experience of transcendentality as gracious gift guards against this danger.

⁸ "Experience of Self and God," *TI* XIII: 125.

⁹ Ibid. See also "Faith between Rationality and Emotion," *TI* XVI, trans. David Morland (New York: Seabury, 1979), p. 67.

¹⁰ "The Concept of Mystery in Catholic Theology," *TI* IV, trans. Kevin Smyth (New York: Seabury, 1966), p. 50.

¹¹ Ibid., p. 51.

¹² "The Experience of God Today," *TI* XI, trans. David Bourke (New York: Seabury, 1974), pp. 157-158. See also Anne Carr, "Starting with the Human," in *A World of Grace,* ed. Leo J. O'Donovan (New York: Seabury, 1980), p. 22 and Bacik, p. 28.

¹³ "Experience of God Today," *TI* XI: 154.

¹⁴ "Faith, Rationality and Emotion," *TI* XVI: 66.

¹⁵ *Foundations,* p. 124. (Although inclusive language has been employed throughout this book, the original language of the quoted material has been retained.)

[16] "Nature and Grace," *TI* IV: 183.

[17] Ibid., pp. 183-184.

[18] "The Development of Dogma," *TI* I, trans. Cornelius Ernst (New York: Seabury, 1961), p. 63.

[19] Ibid., pp. 64-65.

[20] Anne Carr points out that Rahner's work in this area is more than epistemology but "...rather a 'metaphysics of knowledge' in which an affirmation of being is involved in every human judgment." "Theology and Experience in the Thought of Karl Rahner," *Journal of Religion* 53 (1973), 362.

[21] For a helpful discussion of the Kantian influence in *Spirit in the World,* see Francis P. Fiorenza, "Karl Rahner and the Kantian Problematic," in *Spirit in the World,* trans. William Dych (Montreal: Palm Publishers, 1968), pp. xix-xlv.

[22] For a more extended and complete presentation of Rahner's foundational thought in *Spirit in the World,* see Anne Carr, *The Theological Method of Karl Rahner* (Missoula, Montana: Scholars Press, 1977), pp. 59-88.

[23] *Foundations,* p. 17.

[24] Ibid., p. 18.

[25] Ibid., p. 20.

[26] *Spirit in the World,* p. 145.

[27] Fiorenza, "Kantian Problematic," *Spirit in the World,* pp. xxii-xxviii.

[28] *Spirit in the World,* p. 160.

[29] Ibid., p. 158.

[30] "The Development of Dogma," *TI* I: 64. Asymptotically means tending toward the goal but never reaching it.

[31] *Foundations,* p. 15.

[32] Ibid.

[33] Ibid., p. 16.

[34] Ibid., p. 17. See also "Concept of Mystery," *TI* IV: 49-50.

[35] *Foundations,* p. 18.

[36] Ibid., pp. 16-17.

[37] "Concept of Mystery," *TI* IV: 49-50.

[38] "Theology of Symbol," *TI* IV: 230.

[39] Ibid., pp. 236-237.

[40] Ibid., p. 237.

[41] "What Is a Sacrament?" *TI* XIV, trans. David Bourke (New York: Seabury, 1976), nt. 10, pp. 140-141. See also "The Word and the Eucharist," *TI* IV: 253-286.

[42] "What Is a Sacrament?" *TI* XIV: 140.

[43] Rahner, "Dogma," *ET:* 353.

[44] Although foundational to Rahner's understanding of revelation, *Hearers of the Word* has been critiqued for its presentation of revelation as "the objective, official, 'categoreal' reality available in the propositions of the doctrines of the church." Anne Carr notes that very early on Rahner moves beyond this position to the position which I describe in the text, i.e., revelation as primarily transcendental and secondarily, but constitutively, categorical. Metz notes this development in the second edition of *Hearers.* Carr, *Theological Method,* p. 106. See Rahner, *Hearers of the Word,* trans. Michael Richards (Montreal: Palm Publishers, 1969), pp. vii-x.

[45] Karl Rahner and Joseph Ratzinger, *Revelation and Tradition,* trans. W. J. O'Hara (London: Burns and Oates, 1966), pp. 13-14.

[46] Rahner, "Revelation," *ET:* 1462.

[47] *Revelation and Tradition,* pp. 16-17.

[48] *A Rahner Reader,* ed. Gerald A. McCool (New York: Seabury, 1975), p. 64. (From *Hearers of the Word,* Ch. 13.)

CHAPTER 2

Dogma and Revelation

Dogma relates particularly to the categorical dimension of revelation. It is one element of the process by which God's revelation enters into human history. But a prior and fundamental question that needs to be addressed to Rahner's theology before looking specifically at the role of dogma is why there needs to be a history of revelation at all. Rahner asks the question himself:

> If God as he is in himself has already communicated himself in his Holy Spirit always and everywhere and to every person as the innermost center of his existence, whether he wants it or not, whether he reflects upon it or not, whether he accepts it or not, and if the whole history of creation is already borne by God's self-communication in this very creation, then there does not seem to be anything else which can take place on God's part. Then the whole history of salvation and revelation as we understand it in the categorical and particular terms of time and space does not seem to be able to be anything else but the process of limiting and mythologizing and reducing to a human level something which was already present in its fullness from the outset.[1]

The answer, of course, lies for Rahner in the free and historical constitution of the human being as he or she exists in the

world. Because human beings exist in the world, their constitutive
transcendence is always experienced historically. Even human
self-reflection never takes place in a purely a-historical fashion.
It is in the process of knowing external reality that one at the
same time experiences both self and God. God's self-
communication then is never experienced solely as immanent
— as arising totally from human subjectivity. Even God's deepest
self-communication to the human being is experienced only in
contact with worldly reality, though not necessarily with explicitly
religious phenomena. There must be a history of revelation, then,
in the first place, because God's self-communication to human
beings, the fulfillment of their constitutive transcendence, is
always experienced by men and women in their situation in time
and space. In this sense, then, the whole of human history is
a history of revelation.

The historical nature of revelation is also grounded in the
freedom of God and of the human being. God's self-revelation
is free. God could have chosen to remain silent. Men and women
are also free to accept or reject God's constant self-offer to them.
Thus the offer and acceptance or rejection of God's grace are
events occurring in history. The dialectical relationship between
offer and acceptance is most significant. Revelation involves both
God's offer and human acceptance. God's word would be uttered
into a vacuum were not the human being constituted as
essentially receptive to that revelation. ''There is no revelation
which could take place in any other way except in the faith of
the person hearing the revelation.''[2] The human, historical
response, then, as epitomized by ''word'' is present and has co-
constitutive significance for revelation. The recognition that
transcendental revelation has a history provides the foundation
for Rahner's understanding of categorical revelation. Categorical
revelation attempts ''to mediate the original, unreflexive and
non-objective revelation historically, to make it reflexive and to

interpret it in propositions."[3]

Any discussion of revelation which does not include both transcendental and categorical aspects, Rahner would consider incomplete. In one sense, then, categorical revelation may be understood as the human and historical appropriation of, and reflection on, the original transcendental experience of revelation. But it is important to remember in this context that Rahner sees as divine not only the activity of God's self-offer to human beings but also the human activity of response. This too he sees as divinized in a certain sense, or borne by God's grace. "For God, divinizing man through Himself, becomes co-author of the act of 'hearing' (faith), that is, the act which accepts God's self-disclosure and self-communication."[4]

This human activity of hearing in faith grounds Rahner's understanding of categorical revelation, and it is out of this understanding of categorical revelation that his attitude toward dogma grows. The one revelation enters into human history through the mediating activity of the human mind which, elevated by the light of faith, is able to interpret truly and to translate this transcendental experience into the human word. "The historical mediation of this transcendental experience is also revealed as valid, as bringing about and authenticating the absolute experience of God."[5] This mediation of the one revelation in human history, Rahner says, is what is commonly referred to as the history of revelation.

Special Categorical Revelation

Rahner makes some further distinctions in his description of categorical revelation. The dynamism to become explicit in propositional form is universal. All people and all religious traditions have attempted to articulate the religious experience of God's gracious presence. This is true even of those people who would not use conventionally religious terms to describe this experience. So in a general sense the term categorical revelation may be used to describe all attempts to articulate an awareness of the gracious mystery of life. But Rahner also uses the term in a more specialized sense. This he sometimes clarifies by calling it the special history of revelation. "It is helpful to distinguish between the general history of salvation, where religion and God's presence are universally present, and the special history of salvation, a segment of religious history in which we discern a more powerful, a clearer activity and direction by God."[6] This is perhaps what is most commonly understood by the term revelation in itself.

Rahner envisions the history of revelation as moving in a certain direction. The attempts at articulation and clarification which characterize primitive religions, for example, are groping toward a deeper and fuller interpretation of the mystery of God's self-revelation. The fullness of this understanding is reached in the event of Jesus Christ who epitomizes both the complete self-offering of God and its definitive and authentic human acceptance in history. Until this event of Jesus Christ, Rahner says, the history of revelation contained a mixture of authentic interpretation and ambiguity and error. "In Jesus Christ, the crucified and risen one, then, we have a criterion for distinguishing in the concrete history of religion between what is a human misunderstanding of the transcendental experience of God, and what is the legitimate interpretation of this experience. It is only in him that such a discernment of spirits in an ultimate sense is possible."[7]

This pivotal event of Jesus Christ is what enables us to distinguish between a universal categorical revelation — a propositional revelation which contains ambiguity and error — and a special categorical revelation.[8] "This special history then

is really identical with the Old and New Testament history. This
categorical history of revelation in the Old and New Testaments
can and must be understood as the valid self-interpretation of
God's transcendental self-communication to man, and as the
thematization of the universal categorical history of this self-
communication.''[9] A full understanding of revelation, then, for
Rahner, includes transcendental revelation universal categorical
revelation and special categorical revelation. The third aspect
provides the proximate background for Rahner's understanding of dogma so it bears further probing. Once again Rahner
uses the term ''word'' as a key concept. As God's saving action
in history receives its authentic interpretation for the community
one can begin to speak of special categorical revelation. Events
in human history remain ambiguous until they receive
interpretation through the word.[10]

The clearest and most unambiguous instance of this is the
event of Jesus Christ in which action and word are most intimately united. Looking back from the Christ event, Rahner sees
the beginning of the history of this authentic interpretation of
God's action in the Old Testament prophetic tradition which
he uses as a paradigm for the relation of word and event. The
prophet is one who is able to interpret accurately the experience
of God's activity in human life. Not all of us are prophets.
Because of the interdependence among human beings it is often
the case that we must rely on the interpretation of others in order
to arrive at a correct understanding of God's saving activity.
With Jesus Christ, *the* prophet and therefore the ''absolute bringer of salvation,''[11] came the fullness of the prophetic ideal. ''He
is the eschatologically final prophet, *the* prophet as such, who
cannot be surpassed in the further history of revelation and salvation, not because God arbitrarily decided that no prophet (to
surpass him) should be sent, but because his task and his person
are identical . . . . He brings the absolute immediacy and self-

communication of God, not just a particular message and promise.''[12]

With the Christ-event the role of prophecy changed somewhat. Rather than being a vehicle of new revelation, the prophets become ''those who strive to uphold his message in its purity, who attest that message and make it relevant to their day.''[13] After the death and resurrection of Jesus Christ this prophetic role of guarding and formulating and transmitting God's revelation passed to the church. ''The Church itself is the permanent presence of the word of *the* prophet, Jesus Christ. It is the Church in which the word effects what it signifies and is therefore a prophetic word.''[14] The prophetic tradition reveals that there are those who have been given authority to interpret for the community and that their formulations take on a special significance to which individualistic interpretations must often submit. Rahner, of course, recognizes the difficulties involved in assigning this role to the church, and these will be discussed at greater length when we treat the problem of authority in the church more specifically.

Special categorical revelation of its very nature involves free, historical one-time events. It raises the problem of how once-for-all events can be understood to be significant for all time. It involves also the issue of the adequacy and permanence of those formulations and propositions which are the verbal interpretations of those events. Special categorical revelation, beginning with the prophetic tradition, then obviously leads to a consideration of the propositions and formulations in which God's revelation has been articulated in the light of the fundamental event of Jesus Christ.

Early Formulations

From earliest time in Christianity there have been propositions and formulations which purport to interpret God's revelation for the community in an authoritative and lasting way. Within this whole history Rahner situates his discussion of dogma, although the term has come in later centuries to be interpreted in a much narrower fashion. The mediation of revelation in propositions and formulations has taken various forms in the history of revelation. Creeds, kerygma, sacred scripture and theological statements are other forms of doctrinal statements which have important similarities as well as significant differences from dogma narrowly understood. Rahner suggests that the modern distrust of dogma and dogmatic thinking rests on a misunderstanding which absolutizes the differences between it and the other forms of the mediation of revelation mentioned above.

The Earliest Creeds

Contrary to Harnack's contention that dogmatic language is secondary and derivative, a corruption of the "pure" revelatory word of the gospel,[15] Rahner asserts that what may be called "dogmatic thinking" is part of the very fabric of the New Testament. He points out the acknowledged existence of primitive credal formulas which seem to have been part of the early oral tradition that formed the basis for the development of the New Testament. He indicates several interesting features of these credal formulas. They are contained in short confessions of faith such as 1 Corinthians 15:3-5. "For I delivered to you as of first importance what I also received, that Christ died for our sins in accordance with the scriptures, that he was buried, that he was raised on the third day in accordance with the scriptures and that he appeared to Cephas, then to the twelve.'' Other examples include Romans 1:3 and 1 Thessalonians 1:9-10. These confessions oftentimes reflect heterogeneous theological concepts.[16] They have different functions, ''having either a solemn, liturgical, and hymnic character or a more prosaic, catechetical, doctrinal flavor.''[17] And they reflect different local traditions and life situations.[18]

Rahner sees in these formulas a very early emergence of doctrine, that is, of theological reflection on the events of revelation and the development of the need to set forth correct interpretations of these events over against any possible false interpretations. Right from the very beginning, then, even *before* the New Testament writings, there existed, in spite of the differing forms of the various confessions, an attempt at unity of faith. He cites Ephesians 4:5-6 specifically as evidence of this concern: ''One Lord, one faith, one baptism, one God and Father of us all, who is above all and through all and in all.'' He notes the recurrence of various expressions and motifs which indicate that the various credal formulas which were part of the oral tradition had a significant effect on the formation of the New Testament writings.[19] They indicate that the Christian community very early saw the need to interpret the experience of revelation briefly and in terms that would be understood in the intellectual and cultural context of the time. Proclamation involved interpretation.

The variety in these formulations indicates that the verbal formulas themselves varied according to place and traditions, etc., but the effort was always to remain faithful to the events to which these formulas attested. Rahner notes that the fact that these formulas emerged out of the pre-literary tradition exposes them to all the dangers of distortion and error possible in such oral transmission but that in spite of these dangers they preserve the central claim of the revelation event. The significance of this primitive credal tradition Rahner sees not in any material connection between it and the creeds of the early church but in the principles involved. These creeds involved a plurality of attestations to the one message in the language and conceptual framework of the communities out of which they emerged. They tended to be brief and to concentrate on the essentials of faith. They seem to have had as part of their function the setting off of orthodox belief against the false interpretations so possible in those early days before the written testimony of the New Testament. The existence of these creeds as demonstrated by historical-critical biblical exegesis clearly undermines any canonization of the word of scripture as antithetical to the existence of dogma.[20]

Dogma in the New Testament

The confessional formulations containing the early credal statements are just one evidence of dogmatic thinking in the New Testament. The New Testament in general represents the initial attempt at dogmatic thinking on the part of the earliest Christians and thus, as the beginning of the traditioning process, may be seen as the historical foundation and justification for all later dogmatic statements. Far from seeing dogma and gospel as antithetical, Rahner sees dogma as existing in dynamic continuity with scripture.[21]

This location of the dogmatic principle right within the New Testament itself provides a key to his understanding and interpretation of dogma. The New Testament shows clearly the need to translate Christian revelation into words and concepts suitable to particular times and places. It also demonstrates the dangers involved in such interpretative effort and offers some criteria for judging its results. ''The need for a translation of the Christian message into 'modern terms' (which is already shown as necessary by the New Testament itself) shows that by pointing out the dangers of such an undertaking (adapting and falsifying what has been revealed), we might gain the proper criteria for judging such attempts.''[22]

Based on his understanding of scripture, Rahner does not see the criteria for ongoing attempts at reformulation of the message of revelation in establishing a direct relationship of later formulations to the linguistic formulations of the New Testament itself. Rather he sees in the New Testament the earliest and, therefore, pre-eminent interpretation of the Christ-event to which all later interpretations must refer. It is not, therefore, the linguistic formulations themselves that are most important but the reality to which they refer.

The norm for further dogmatic development, consequently, is not the formulations in themselves but those formulations in relationship to the event which they attempt to describe. In looking to the New Testament as a norm for dogmatic assertions, therefore, one must see such assertions as verbal formulations attempting to express a reality which is always greater than any attempt to express it. An inherent quality of human words is that they always contain within themselves more meaning than is able to be comprehended at any one time. ''Every word suggests also what it contains that is unsaid. . .it carries a superfluity of meaning which is not actually knowable at every moment. . .This property of the human word appears most fully in the 'word of God in the human mouth', where to a far higher degree an infinity of meaning to be interpreted is presented in a finite way.''[23] Thus the New Testament provides a paradigm and direction for further statements rather than any fixed and final formulation. The process of appropriating and interpreting revelation is an ongoing one. Scripture is the primordial moment in the process of reflection on revelation which is continued in the dogmatic tradition in the church. The fact of dogmatic development even within the New Testament is of course a presupposition of Rahner's understanding of development of dogma.

An important principle for Rahner is that the ongoing "dogmatic thinking through" of the events of revelation takes place not only in contact with the normative and earliest preserved interpretation of these events, the New Testament, but also in contact with the continuing history of their interpretation in the tradition of the church. Rahner continues to believe that any contemporary articulation of faith must take into consideration and be limited by all previous articulations.[24] This is in spite of an increasing tendency even among Roman Catholic theologians to consult primarily, if not only, the New Testament as a criterion for the validity of doctrinal statements.

The inclusion of scripture *within* tradition rather than as an external norm to it provides another important principle for Rahner's understanding of dogma. The word is and has from the beginning been handed on in the church. Its authority is not guaranteed by an external imposition of authority but grows out of the relationship of word and apostolic succession in the church. "The succession is accepting the service of the word, it is testimony to the message that has been entrusted to it. 'Succession means holding fast to the apostolic word, as tradition means the continued existence of authorized witnesses.' "[25] So authority in the church comes from adherence to the word. Word and office are not two entirely different realities, externally related to each other, but exist from the beginning in interdependence. "The 'matter' of the 'gospel' and the authority of the word which is manifested in Church doctrine are not two separate entities which are afterwards brought together in a further operation."[26] By his discussion of the relationship of the New Testament to dogma Rahner attempts to diffuse two of the main objections against dogma, that it distorts scripture and is arbitrarily imposed by external authority. He shows that dogmatic thinking is rooted in scripture and is intrinsically related to authority in the church as it developed from the relationship of word and apostolic succession.

The Nature and Function of Dogma

Thus far we have been working with a wide definition of dogma as any kind of doctrinal statement proposed by the church for belief by the faithful. In fact the notion of dogma which has been subject to particular attack in modern times involves a much narrower understanding. Rahner situates this narrower concept within the context of a wider and older view as a way of breaking open the meaning of dogma and discovering new possibilities for contemporary understandings.

According to Rahner, the term dogma has come to connote in the modern world "the idea of a rigid doctrinal system, of constraint of conscience, of high-sounding statements containing venerable ideas which have nonetheless become so far removed from the original Gospel that they appear to conceal belief rather than reveal it."[27] It was not until the eighteenth century that dogma took on the restricted meaning which led to these popular notions. This concept of dogma represents a considerable restriction of the range of meanings which dogma encompassed in the first centuries of Christianity and into medieval times.

Medieval theologians, according to Rahner, used the word dogma very little, preferring the word *articulus* to refer to what we today call dogma. More important than this use or non-use of the word, however, is the difference in attitude toward the reality to which it refers. For the medieval theologian, the primary attribute of dogma was *not* the demand for obedience to external authority. " 'Dogma,' for St. Thomas, is not determined by the 'objective' boundaries of a pure *'fides divina'* and qualified by the question of the theological *degree of certainty,* rather is its correspondence with belief equally part of the doctrinal character of dogma. The significance of what is to be believed is an important element of dogma."[28] So for medieval theologians, epitomized by Thomas, dogma was characterized by the significance of its content, at least to some extent, if not more than by the authority which guaranteed it.

It was not until much later when dogma and tradition were challenged that the necessity of distinguishing and regulating various expressions of faith became necessary. The term dogma, then, was not always defined in Christian history in the narrow sense which has become so problematic in modern times. Dogma was not always understood to derive its authority purely from an external source. It rather primarily derived its claim for obedience from its intrinsic connection to the Christian mystery (i.e., as expressed in Christian creeds and New Testament statements).

In a development given new impetus at the reformation, with its emphasis on scripture as the norm of right belief, and culminating in the eighteenth century, dogma began to take on the narrower sense to which we have become accustomed. Until then there had been no need to tie down its meaning because its existence was so taken for granted that it seldom became an object of reflection. "That had to change the moment that this belief was attacked at the root, in its hidden certainty, reliability, and automatic force, when the new and dangerous heresies emerged at the beginning of the thirteenth century."[29] The defining process culminated in the eighteenth century. Vatican I adopted this eighteenth century view and thus it became the official as well as the popular understanding of the term which has endured to the present.

At Vatican I a distinction was clearly drawn between the

deposit of faith and the dogmas of the church.[30] "The word of God is divine, absolute, inexhaustible; but dogma in this new sense is a human and finite statement by the Church concerning the *depositum fidei.*"[31] In this view dogma relies for its claim to obedience on its juridical imposition by the magisterium. It is presented for belief by either the ordinary or the extraordinary magisterium of the church. The most formal presentation of a dogma is called a definition. "In the strict sense, therefore, dogma implies the final decision through a solemn 'definition' which has at the same time the quality of a canonical ruling of the Church. Its denial is regarded by the Church as 'heresy' and is anathematized."[32]

Vatican I's definition of infallibility is a logical development of such a view of dogma and is related to the understanding of dogmas primarily as lists of propositions to be believed. Rahner's reaction to Vatican I's view of dogma is in fact a good illustration of his method of dealing with past doctrinal assertions. He in no way asserts that its view of dogma is false, but he does say that it is a one-sided view and thus although it may truly describe one aspect of dogma, it should not be understood as a full definition of the term.[33] He counsels a return to the sources in order to recover a fuller understanding of the word dogma in its many dimensions, one that would not be so objectionable to contemporary people. He includes the earlier and more all-encompassing understandings prevalent until the reformation, particularly emphasizing the religious significance of dogma which occupies a central place in St. Thomas's view. The emphasis on the *content* of dogma Rahner restores to its rightful position as an important determining characteristic of dogma. It is not only the formal correctness of dogma or its imposition by legitimate authority that calls forth assent, but also the significance of its content. This has important implications for his understanding of the role of the teaching office in the church.

What Is a Dogmatic Statement?

In his article entitled "What Is a Dogmatic Statement?"[34] Rahner enumerates the complex ingredients that make up a dogmatic statement. The nature of such a statement involves far more than an externally imposed obligation to believe in certain propositions. To understand dogmatic statements fully, Rahner says, one must see them in their similarities and differences from other types of human statements.

A human statement. Dogmatic statements involve a claim to be true in the ordinary sense in which human statements make that claim. Since the dogmatic statement shares the structure of any human statement there are certain characteristics which must be taken into account in any hermeneutical endeavor, i.e., "the relation to the person making the statement, the historical nature of the conceptual elements, the involvement in a historical and sociological context, a logical structure, a variety of literary forms and types, unknown and unconsciously shared areas and affinities of experience between the speaker and the listeners without which there could be no real possibility of understanding and agreement."[35] An approach such as Denzinger which merely lists propositions out of context isolates the individual proposition and canonizes it. Rahner makes clear that the belief claim of dogmatic statements does not make them any less fully human statements, in need of interpretation to be understood in new contexts.

A true statement. Secondly, the truth claim of a dogmatic statement does not merely rest on its successful articulation of the subjective state of the speaker. Obviously referring to and rejecting the so-called modernist conception, Rahner insists that a dogmatic statement refers to and attempts to articulate a reality which is essentially outside itself. A formulation cannot be considered both true and false at the same time, since it is not just an attempt to describe a unique subjective experience, but rather to describe a reality which exists independently of the attempt to know and describe it. There can, however, be a possible disjunction between one's pre-conceptual apprehension of a reality and one's ability to articulate that reality truly which makes it very difficult to judge from the outside a person's grasp of the truths of Christianity. One could conceivably grasp the truth accurately at the pre-propositional level and articulate it falsely (in which case, according to Rahner, one would be saved) or conversely one could have a false or inadequate pre-conceptual grasp of a truth but could articulate it in the conventional and acceptable way. The person who learned catechism answers by rote but never recognized the implications of these truths for daily living might be an example of this.

The analogous nature of dogmatic statements should also be recognized in their interpretation, but this should not lead to mere agnosticism about the ultimate reality to which dogmatic statements refer. Analogy should be understood in its traditional Roman Catholic theological sense when referring to the Absolute. ''For even what is unexperienced still has an objective likeness to what is experienced, and the transcendental affirmation of a similarity of analogy, in spite of the greater dissimilarity which obtains between divine and finite reality, belongs to those original intellectual data which are implicitly reaffirmed in every affirmation and negation.''[36] Such an understanding of analogy reinforces Rahner's contention, referred to above, that dogmatic statements are not merely subjective and, therefore, possibly both true and false at the same time, but that in fact they involve a claim to be true.

Having said this, however, Rahner goes on to insist that truth and falsity are not the only possible properties of human statements. Here he attempts to respond to some of the criticism against dogma by asserting that in spite of being true, dogmas may at the same time be inopportune, historically inappropriate — in other words sinful and guilty. This is an important point for Rahner. By being true, dogmatic statements are not removed from the human situation which, while being graced, at the same time remains guilty and sinful. It is possible to critique such propositions from the point of view of appropriateness, to ask whether they are not in fact at a certain historical moment more a hindrance than a help to personal faith. And it is possible to make this critique without challenging their objective claim to truth.

A faith statement. A dogmatic statement is further qualified by being a statement of faith. This assertion has a number of implications. First the dogmatic statement is a statement of faith because it arises essentially out of the aspect of listening with its correlative, reflection, which belongs to the act of faith. "A first basic 'theological' reflection takes place in the merely obedient listening to the word of God. That means, however, that dogmatic reflexion and its statement can and must never be completely separated from its own origin: from faith itself in its character as an act."[37]

This has important implications for the understanding of dogmatic statements since it implies that the unbeliever and the believer will not have the same experience in approaching a dogmatic statement. The believer approaches it from within the "light of faith." "The profane student of religion does not automatically see a dogmatic statement in the same way as a theologian does. The insight which is conveyed in it is determined before its actual articulation in the statement by the act of the person who accepts or rejects grace."[38] Thus the dogmatic statement is not merely a reflection on the event of salvation but, when heard within the light of faith, brings one directly into the heart of that event.

An ecclesial statement. It is the ecclesial character of dogmatic statements which most clearly differentiates them from other types of theological statements. This character arises out of two main factors: (1) the communal and historical nature of the human situation and (2) the once-for-all nature of the salvation event. Dogmatic statements grow out of the need for reflection and expression of the once-for-all event of salvation in common and contemporary terms. Because human beings are historical, there must be theology and this theology must have at least the possibility of being a binding statement of the events of salvation.

Although all theology, even that of an individual, bears a relationship to the church in that it is at least in dialogue, even as question or critique, with the church's teaching, Rahner points out that there is an even more strongly ecclesiological theology ''in which the Church as a whole engages in theological activity through the bearers of her established *magisterium.*''[39] For Rahner, one of the claims to authority of dogmatic statements arises out of the fact that in dogmatic statements we have the church doing theology and not just individuals. Because the church is the authorized interpreter of God's revelation in history, the church can command obedience to such statements. This does not empower the church to proclaim a new revelation but to offer binding interpretations of the one revelation for different historical periods.

In this understanding, dogmatic statements represent the fullest possibility of theological statements in general. Thus, theology, in its fullest possibility as dogma, is not merely a second-ary and human interpretation of revelation but in fact is the concrete presence of that revelation today. Rahner states this very strongly. ''This theology is also a real proclamation of faith which demands obedience inasmuch as the Church, in its teaching authority, can make the claim that its Gospel, thus constituted, that is, transformed into theology, *is* (and is not just *about*) the form, valid here and now, of the word in which God has spoken to us."[40]

Dogma and the Magisterium: Dogma, Authority and Freedom

The issue of the church's right to demand obedience to its dogmatic statements is one of the most controversial aspects of the contemporary debate over dogma. Dogma does not, in Rahner's eyes, receive its authority purely extrinsically from having been proclaimed authoritatively by the magisterium. What then is the source of the authority attached to dogmatic statements? How can an authoritative magisterium be reconciled with human freedom?

Rahner's efforts to clarify the nature of dogmatic statements and their relationship to revelation represent an attempt to break out of the narrow juridical context in which dogma had been viewed particularly since Vatican I. In the minds of many Catholics faith was equated with adherence to the dogmas which were proposed for belief by the magisterium, or teaching authority of the church. One of the "advantages" of being a Catholic was the absolute certainty one could have about doctrines because of their guarantee by the church's infallible teaching magisterium. Nor has this attitude completely disappeared.

Some Catholics assuredly find such certainty consoling. In many ways it is easier to avoid personal responsibility and to accept truths blindly on the authority of another. Others, Catholics as well as critics of religion from outside the Catholic Church, have found this understanding of dogma, as obedience to external authority, the major stumbling block to the acceptance of the idea of dogma and of dogmatic religion. Today many rebel against the idea of accepting things "on faith." In a rational and scientific age people feel the need to grapple with decisions of faith through the use of their own mental processes. To be asked to accept doctrines on the authority of the church is deemed to be an insult to "human beings come of age."

Thus although there remain those who find it safer and easier to abdicate the responsibility for their own lives to the teaching authority of the church and to live a life of faith equated with obedience, many find such a view of religion increasingly problematic. For them dogma has become a sign of what they see as a radical abuse of human freedom and dignity. Dogma should play no part in the contemporary religion of enlightened humankind. Nor should the magisterium of the church have the power to impose such dogmas on Catholics today.

Rahner is sympathetic to this critique but suggests that it rests on an inadequate understanding of dogma and a misconception of the role of the magisterium in the church (although a misconception often reinforced by the attitudes and actions of those actually exercising the teaching office in the church). Dogma, as noted above, involves far more than its merely juridical elements. In Rahner's understanding, contrary to the widely held misconceptions of the past and present, persons should not be asked to assent to dogma purely on the grounds of its presentation by the formal authority of the church.[41] This conviction is grounded in his theology of freedom.

The Relationship of Freedom and Legitimate Authority

A primary datum of Rahner's theology is his understanding of the human being as a free being capable of self-determination.[42] "Freedom is. . .the capacity to make oneself once and for all, the capacity which of its nature is directed towards the freely willed finality of the subject as such . . . The free person must answer for himself and the totality of his life before the judgment seat of God."[43] Characteristic of Rahner's view of Christian freedom is his insistence that freedom includes not only the possibility of saying yes to one's existence and thus also to God but also the possibility of a definitive no. Because of the always present offer of God's grace, however, the balance is tipped toward affirmation rather than denial. This is the basic meaning of freedom for Rahner, freedom as a transcendental characteristic of human existence. "Freedom is first of all 'freedom of being.' "[44] The primary meaning of freedom then is not the unfettered capacity to choose one object from among others but the ability ultimately to choose or to reject God within one's humanly limited situation of guilt and determination.

Of course this ultimate, or transcendental, freedom is a process which is concretized in the many actual decisions one makes within one's limited human situation. This is categorical freedom. This understanding of freedom has great implications for Rahner's views on dogma and the magisterium. If freedom is ultimately self-determination, in the sense and with the limitations described above, then one's religious life as a whole cannot be predicated on unreflective acceptance of truths on the authority of another, even if that other is the teaching authority of the church. Ultimately the responsibility for one's relationship with God rests with one's own freely determined acceptance of one's own human existence and this is prior (not always in a temporal sense) to any confrontation with the church's teaching.

Freedom and the Church's Teaching

Since transcendental freedom is primary, one can accept some limitations on one's categorical freedom without violating that basic freedom which is a human existential. "Anyone who, having been set free for his freedom to be engaged in infinite hope, accepts the limitations imposed upon his freedom at the social level by all the institutions to which he is subject (and in fact, of course, without making this liberation of his grounds for an unjustifiable conservatism and social petrification), is living for God in a spirit of faith and hope.''[45] The parenthesis in this quotation is important to avoid an interpretation of such a view as offering an ''opiate'' for the people, as suggesting that one can live in a human situation of unfreedom in the light of a transcendental but not yet achieved freedom. This Rahner does not suggest.

He rather implies that the actualization of one's transcendental freedom comes about in the efforts to overcome those unfreedoms which will always impinge upon our lives. Since human life is a dialectic in which the effort to overcome some unfreedom often leads to the imposition of new restrictions, our lives will never be totally without external limitations on freedom. But it is the ongoing attempt to promote freedom within these situations which leads to that transcendental freedom that is the goal of human life. Paradoxically, institutions, and here the church and its teaching authority can be included, are usually set up to safeguard freedom but in the process they also limit it. By this limitation, however, they actually call forth freedom by the protest against limitations which they bring about.[46] In the church as institution, therefore, and in its teaching authority and its doctrine, which are part of this institutional element, there is a tension between freedom and limitations. To accept the ongoing presence of this dialectic, however, is not to adopt a passive stance toward it. ''This dialectical unity between manipulation and freedom in the Church is not, however, a static polarity of two always equal factors. It implies a history of freedom and a task to fight for freedom. Even in the Church it is always necessary to fight again and again for this space for freedom, to define it repeatedly and if possible to enlarge it.''[47]

Rahner's view of transcendental freedom then provides the

basis for his view of the right of the individual to freedom in the concrete circumstances of his or her life. "This view of freedom must be the foundation of the doctrine of a rightly understood freedom of conscience and of the right of freedom to room for its concrete realization in face of undue restrictions laid upon it by State or Church."[48] He applies this insight concretely to dogma and the teaching office of the church. The area of the expression of the church's teaching is co-determined by freedom and manipulation. There may be manipulation on the part of the church's teaching office whether intentional or unintentional. In the past, however, this was often not acknowledged, leaving Catholics and critics of Catholicism with the impression that what was expected by the church was a blind childish obedience. The church must now acknowledge the legitimate sphere of freedom belonging to Catholics or risk the loss of faith of many who, living in an "enlightened" world, can no longer accept a faith purely on the word of another. This acknowledgement is no mere concession to the modern world, says Rahner, but in fact represents a more authentic and traditional understanding of the teaching office and of dogma.

All Christians according to Rahner "now have some room for freedom so that they can freely decide about the truth with regard to the official teaching of the Church....They have it [freedom] in the first place with regard to the Church's dogma, insofar as they cannot be compelled to believe and cannot be punished for not believing by any social pressure from the Church."[49] Obviously Catholics have this same freedom with respect to non-definitive but authentic pronouncements of the church's teaching office. Because the existence of this freedom is not yet recognized by all the authorities in the church, Rahner says there must be a deliberate effort to bring about an acknowledgement of this freedom in the church. To that end "the authority of the Church, its pastoral office and *potestas iurisdictionis* must be reinterpreted."[50]

This reinterpretation must take place, he says, within the continuing conviction that authority, office, power and office bearers have a role in the church. He also accepts as a guideline for reinterpretation that the substance of faith is binding and constitutive of the church and that the church's proclamation of that message is authoritative. The substance of faith is rooted in a deeper reality but the doctrinal propositional content of that faith, rightly understood, is also constitutive of faith.[51] Because of this, if a person with full understanding and as an ultimate personal decision contradicts a dogma of the church, the church as an institution may call public attention to the fact that that person has chosen to separate himself or herself from the church. This choice in itself, however, is an act of freedom since it is the free decision of a person to belong or not to belong to the church. (This freedom was often not acknowledged in earlier times when culture or upbringing dictated one's membership in the church and when salvation was predicated on one's explicit membership in the church.)

In actual fact, however, Rahner thinks that it is not often that a person would have to make such an absolute decision about a specific dogma. Most often people's questions and critiques about dogma can be understood as opinions, or as arising from misunderstanding of the dogma. Often also today's debates do not concern teachings that have been formally proposed as dogmas according to the strict criteria, but rather teachings that can be characterized as authentic but non-infallible teachings. Examples of such teachings are the encyclical *Humanae Vitae* (1968) and the "Declaration on the Question of the Admission of Women to the Ministerial Priesthood" (1976). Rahner sees such teachings as open to revision and reform and thus to continuing critical discussion within the church. He says that the present-day views of women and their history of discrimination within the church are essential to the ongoing reexamination of these questions.[52] In Chapter 4 the more pastoral question of the various degrees of acceptance which people may have of the dogmas of the church will be taken up.

Toward a Renewed Magisterium

According to Rahner, a proper understanding of the magisterium should not begin with its authority to teach abstract doctrines. It should rather begin by emphasizing its rootedness in the eschatological victory of the Christ-event. The word which testifies to this event is part of the event itself and this word continues to be uttered in history through the church. It is proclaimed by all its members but, as historically constituted, the church has a confession of faith and a doctrinal authority. This doctrinal authority is only understandable as a witness to the continuing presence of the truth of Christ in the whole community.[53] The function of the teaching office "is conceivable only as one aspect of the eschatologically indestructible community of faith. It does not supervene from outside, by means of an authorisation which is simply conceived of in juridical terms."[54] This is Rahner's basic justification for the notion of an "infallible" magisterium. "The Church would not be the eschatological community of salvation if it were not in 'infallible' possession of the truth of Christ."[55] The infallibility of the teaching office is thus rooted in and is a part of the whole Christian community.

Acceptance of the existence of binding and true propositions of faith rests on the supposition that such statements are in essence verbalizations by the church of the *one* revelation and participate in the truth of that revelation because of the continuing presence of Christ in the church. It is thus more correct to speak of the charism of infallibility as belonging to the church and manifesting itself in the legitimate bearers of its authority than it is to speak of infallible propositions.

Although the teaching office is legitimated by its connection to the Christ-event, it is subject to certain limitations which Rahner says are not always recognized either by those in authority or by the average Catholic.

First, the ultimate ground of faith is *not* the teaching office. The infallibility of the magisterium is a secondary datum in the hierarchy of truths.[56] The primary act of faith for all human beings must come from their ultimate trust in and acceptance of existence. Only on the basis of this fundamental trust in the gracious mystery, which for Christians reaches definitive expression in Jesus Christ, can one come to accept the meaning and function of the church and its teaching office. It is this basic trust that grounds one's acceptance of the authority of the church and not vice versa.

In terms of freedom, then, the teaching authority of the church is not, as it is sometimes understood, an escape from the need to take personal responsibility for decisions of faith. "The existence and justification of the Church's teaching office is something which each individual must in fact recognize and accept as such *without* being able to base himself on the authority of this teaching office. In other words he must act solely 'at his own risk.' "[57] The acceptance of the authority of the teaching office is itself a free act of faith. Acceptance of the teaching authority of the church never dispenses one from the ongoing need to reaffirm that free act of basic trust which is prior to any acceptance of the teaching office or the individual teachings of that office. In fact both the teaching authority of the church and any decisions which it makes should be understood as articulations of the essence of Christian faith to which Christians have already assented as a prior condition for their acceptance of the teaching authority. "In any definitorial decisions which these representatives of the teaching office arrive at, the Church's own absolute assent of faith as worked out in history, albeit unreflectingly, must already have gone before, so that in a case of this kind the specific charism of the teaching office consists, strictly speaking, in its 'infallible' confirmation of this absolute assent of faith on the part of the Church as a whole, which has already been arrived at."[58]

Because of the secondary nature of the formal authority of the teaching office, Rahner says, it is an increasing responsibility of those who teach in the church not to make declarations which claim assent solely on their formal authority. In the past the formal authority of the teaching office was often conceived of as almost independent of the actual truth of the content to which it attested. This split must be overcome in a renewed magisterium. It must be seen that the formal authority of the teaching office is closely connected to the authority of the content which it proclaims. "Even in the Church there is an authority of 'the thing itself.' "[59] Teachers in the church must be careful to explicate the connection of their proclamation to the authority inherent in the realities it proclaims. They must never ask assent purely on the basis of formal authority. "It can be stated absolutely as a matter of principle that in its individual decisions and the preliminary proposals leading up to these the teaching office of the Church acts best and most correctly when it allows the truth which is sustained by grace and inherent in the reality itself which it is treating of and seeking to teach to make its own impact, and allows its own formal authority almost completely to be effaced by giving pride of place to this truth."[60]

The teaching office in today's church has the responsibility to give reasons for its decisions. It can no longer assume that Catholics are an "obedient flock" for whom a declaration based on formal authority would suffice. "Today, more than in earlier

times, they must see to it, not only that they are right, but also
that they are seen to be right. They ought to present their
authority in a more living and primal way, deriving it from the
centre of Christian faith. They ought to interpret their authority
to contemporary believers persuasively."[61] Free human beings
have the right to clear reasons for what they are asked to believe.
"Freedom of conscience...has got to be respected absolutely,
in matters of religion and the relation of the individual to the
Church as much as elsewhere. This means that the only
permissible means of convincing a human being on a religious
matter is argument."[62]

Rahner, thus, interprets the teaching office of the church
in its function of proclaiming dogma and other truths of faith
in such a way as to make clear and safeguard the sphere of
freedom which is essential to being human. Human beings should
not be asked to accept dogmas or other truths of faith purely
on the formal authority of the magisterium.

And what of the magisterium in the future? Rahner says
that ideally the role of the magisterium will be to render itself,
in a certain sense, superfluous.[63] It will be less focused on further
explicitation of the faith and more on safeguarding and
interpreting its central core. Since it is recognized as a secondary
datum, its role in the ongoing history of faith should be a more
modest one — clearly bearing witness to the more central truths
to which it attests.[64]

In a renewed understanding of the role of the magisterium,
Rahner says, there might be room for an expansion of the idea
of teaching authority to include, along with the pope and bishops,
theologians and other qualified lay people. There might even be
some room for the exercise of more democracy in this sphere
of the church's life. Perhaps, he says, a renewed and expanded
teaching authority might come to its decisions by means of a
vote (with certain provisos distinguishing such a vote from that

in the purely secular arena). "Some form of democratic collaboration in the decisions taken by the teaching office as such in the Church is not impossible from the outset . . . . It is in principle possible from the outset to accord a far wider sphere for such democratic collaboration to be exercised."[65] Rahner thus sees a renewed teaching authority in the future as allowing even more space for the exercise of freedom with respect to the doctrine of the church.

Finally, even when one does basically accept the magisterium and its right to teach authoritatively, within the limits described above, this does not absolve one from the need to have a critical attitude to the church and its dogmas. "*Absolute* assent to a proposition and an abiding attitude of criticism with regard to it are not mutually exclusive."[66] In fact, Rahner says, a critical attitude is required of every Christian, a critical attitude which grows out of and is supported by that basic commitment which is primary and grounds all relationship to the propositional content of faith. It is this absolute commitment at the most fundamental level of existence which gives Christians their ultimate freedom with respect to the dogma of the church. Rahner would thus respond to the often heard dichotomy "dogma *or* freedom" by assuring us that, rightly understood, one can have dogma *and* freedom in the church. He is not so naive as to think that this has always been the case or even that it is at the present time. It is an ideal to work for in the renewed church of the future.

Rahner thus sees authentic formulations of faith as having been part of the church's tradition from earliest times. He sees them as legitimate and necessary to the ongoing attempt to interpret the experience of the incomprehensible mystery and its definitive expression in Jesus Christ. He widens the narrow understanding of dogma which has become increasingly problematic in recent times by retrieving essential elements of dogma which go beyond mere obedience to external authority. Finally, he offers hope for a future exercise of the magisterium where dogma might be more authentically understood and human freedom more clearly respected.

Notes

[1] *Foundations,* p. 139.

[2] Ibid., p. 142. Dermot Lane provides a brief and helpful summary of various theories of revelation, both traditional and contemporary, in *The Experience of God,* pp. 28-49. It provides a useful context for situating Rahner's contribution. For a more extended survey, see Avery Dulles, *Models of Revelation* (New York: Doubleday, 1983).

[3] *Foundations,* p. 173.

[4] "Revelation," *Dictionary of Theology,* 2nd ed., ed. Karl Rahner and Herbert Vorgrimler (New York: Crossroad, 1981), p. 446.

[5] Rahner, "Revelation," *ET:* 1461-1462.

[6] Thomas O'Meara, "A History of Grace," in *World of Grace,* p. 85. This article includes a helpful discussion of the relationship of special categorical revelation to the history of religions in general.

[7] *Foundations,* p. 157. See also p. 175.

[8] For a further discussion of the implications of this idea, see "History of the World and Salvation-History," *TI* V, trans. Karl-H. Kruger (New York: Seabury, 1966), pp. 97-114.

[9] *Foundations,* p. 158.

[10] For further discussion of Rahner's distinction of profane history from salvation history through the interpreting word, see "History of the World and Salvation-History," *TI* V, pp. 106-107.

[11] Rahner, "Prophetism," *ET:* 1288.

[12] Ibid.

[13] Ibid.

[14] Ibid.

[15] See Harnack's attempt to differentiate the essential "kernel" of Christianity from its later expression in dogmatic

religion. *History of Dogma,* 4 vols., translated from the 3rd German edition by Neil Buchanan (New York: Dover Publications, 1961), I: 74-75.

[16] *Kerygma and Dogma,* pp. 50-51.

[17] Ibid., p. 50.

[18] Ibid., p. 51.

[19] Ibid., p. 75.

[20] Today this recognition is not limited to Rahner and other Catholic theologians. Pannenberg and Schlink in two significant articles on dogma from the Protestant tradition agree in seeing evidence of dogmatic thinking within the New Testament itself. Pannenberg, "What Is A Dogmatic Statement?" in *Basic Questions in Theology* I, trans. George H. Kehm (Philadelphia: Fortress Press, 1970). Schlink, "The Structure of Dogmatic Statements as an Ecumenical Problem," in *The Coming Christ and the Coming Church* (London: Oliver and Boyd, 1967), pp. 16-84.

[21] *Kerygma and Dogma,* p. 69.

[22] Ibid., p. 53.

[23] Ibid., p. 70.

[24] Rahner, "Dogma," *ET:* 361.

[25] *Kerygma and Dogma,* p. 79. Included in this quotation is a citation from J. Ratzinger and K. Rahner, *Episcopat und Primat* (Freiburg, 1963), p. 46.

[26] *Kerygma and Dogma,* p. 80.

[27] Ibid., p. 27.

[28] Ibid., p. 29.

[29] Ibid., p. 33.

[30] Ibid., p. 35.

[31] Ibid., pp. 36-37.

[32] Ibid., p. 37.

[33] Ibid., p. 39.

[34] "What Is a Dogmatic Statement?" *TI* V: 42-66.

[35] *Kerygma and Dogma,* p. 82.

³⁶ "What Is a Dogmatic Statement?" *TI* V: 47.

³⁷ *Kerygma and Dogma,* p. 88.

³⁸ Ibid., p. 89.

³⁹ "What Is a Dogmatic Statement?" *TI* V: 53.

⁴⁰ *Kerygma and Dogma,* pp. 91-92.

⁴¹ Rahner's comment on a famous saying of Augustine illustrates his conviction in this regard. "Augustine is quite wrong when he says that he would not believe the gospel if he had not been prompted to do so by the authority of the Church." "Does the Church Offer Any Ultimate Certainties?" *TI* XIV: 51.

⁴² The notion of freedom is very central to Rahner's theology and as such has been much commented on. For good presentations, see Bacik, *Apologetics,* pp. 84-103, and Brian McDermott, "The Bonds of Freedom," in *World of Grace,* pp. 50-63.

⁴³ "Theology of Freedom," *TI* VI, trans. Karl-H. and Boniface Kruger (Baltimore: Helicon Press, 1969), p. 183.

⁴⁴ Ibid., p. 184.

⁴⁵ "Institution and Freedom," *TI* XIII: 119.

⁴⁶ Ibid., p. 105-121.

⁴⁷ Karl Rahner, *Meditations on Freedom and the Spirit,* trans. Rosaleen Ochenden, David Smith and Cecily Bennett (New York: Seabury, 1977), p. 60.

⁴⁸ Rahner, "Freedom," *ET:* 545.

⁴⁹ *Meditations on Freedom and the Spirit,* p. 64. See also p. 60, where Rahner notes that the church is the universal sacrament of freedom and should safeguard and extend freedom in its social sphere.

⁵⁰ Ibid., p. 67.

⁵¹ "Does the Church Offer Any Ultimate Certainties?" *TI* XIV: 57.

⁵² "Women and the Priesthood," *TI* XX, trans. Edward Quinn (New York: Crossroad, 1981), pp. 45-47.

⁵³ Rahner, "Magisterium," *ET* 872. See Michael A. Fahey, "On Being Christian — Together," in *World of Grace,* 134-136, for a clear exposition of how Rahner's view of the authority of the teaching office follows from his understanding of Church as "an expression of the ongoing presence and historical tangibility of God's ultimate and victorious power in Jesus Christ" (p. 134).

⁵⁴ " 'Mysterium Ecclesiae,' " *TI* XVII, trans. Margaret Kohl (New York: Crossroad, 1981), p. 145.

⁵⁵ Rahner, "Magisterium," *ET* 873.

⁵⁶ "The Teaching Office of the Church in the Present-Day Crisis of Authority," *TI* XII, trans. David Bourke (New York: Seabury, 1974), pp. 23-24.

⁵⁷ "The Dispute Concerning the Church's Teaching Office," *TI* XIV: 95.

⁵⁸ "Teaching Office of the Church," *TI* XII: 11.

⁵⁹ " 'Mysterium Ecclesiae,' " *TI* XVII: 144.

⁶⁰ "Teaching Office of the Church," *TI* XII: 26.

⁶¹ " 'Mysterium Ecclesiae,' " *TI* XVII: 146.

⁶² *Meditations on Freedom and the Spirit,* p. 86.

⁶³ "Teaching Office of the Church," *TI* XII: 28.

⁶⁴ "On the Concept of Infallibility in Catholic Theology," *TI* XIV: 75.

⁶⁵ "Teaching Office of the Church," *TI* XII: 20. See pp. 13-22 of this same article for a more extended discussion of the possibilities of more democratic procedures in the church's teaching office.

⁶⁶ "On the Concept of Infallibility," *TI* XIV: 67.

CHAPTER 3

The Development of Dogma

Dogmatic development is an aspect of the issue of dogma that has raised particular problems for the Roman Catholic tradition. It has been a consistent concern in Rahner's writings. The early articles attempt to break open the past question of development for wider discussion while the later offer a vision of dogmatic development for the present and future of the post-Vatican II church.

How the once-for-all decisive event of Jesus Christ continues to be present through history in the doctrine of the church is what constitutes the problem of development of dogma. "All theories of the development of dogmas and of the history of dogmas are nothing other than attempts to give a more exact answer to this question of how a really new truth can be the old truth."[1]

This is a relatively recent problem since its recognition stems from the advent of modern historiography.[2] Not until the nineteenth century did theologians seriously begin to wonder about the apparent discrepancies between the body of doctrine proposed for belief in modern times, especially in the Roman church, and the more limited doctrines of the primitive church, particularly the normative texts of sacred scripture. As mentioned above, Adolph Harnack's famous attempt to deal with this issue saw all doctrines later than the first scriptural witness as accretions which obscured the clear witness of the gospel. Since Harnack, Protestant attempts to deal with the issue have revolved around the science or art of hermeneutics — the attempt to understand past texts in their various contexts and thus to translate the meaning of the text from one cultural or social situation to another.

Catholic attempts have generally, until the very recent past, taken form as theories of development of dogma.[3] Since at the end of the nineteenth and the beginning of this century the official Roman Catholic Church still refused to accept the possibility that its dogmas had developed through history, it was the first task of Roman Catholic theologians to try to bring the church to an acceptance of the very fact of development itself. This recognition involved an acceptance of contemporary historical research.[4] The second task for these theologians was to combat the charge of Harnack and others that these developments had been deleterious to Christian faith.

Alfred Loisy, George Tyrrell and Maurice Blondel were among those early thinkers, in addition to Cardinal Newman, who tried to convince the Roman Catholic Church that to accept the fact of development was not to deny the substantial identity of the nineteenth and twentieth century Roman Catholic Church with the apostolic church. These writers, although each with distinctive emphases, all attempted to make a case for the use of the historical method in the study of doctrine because they recognized the need for the Catholic Church to come to grips with the nineteenth century historical critique of dogma. Their efforts helped lead to the characterization of Loisy and Tyrrell as "modernists."

Their views, with the exception of Tyrrell, see doctrinal development as an essentially positive and progressive movement. Perhaps because of the apologetic intent growing out of their need, in different circumstances, to defend Roman Catholicism from the charge of corruption, Newman, Blondel and Loisy all take an extremely positive view of the consequences of development. Today Loisy sounds a little naive when we read: "The Church became, at important moments, what it had to become in order not to decline and perish, dragging the Gospel down with it."[5] Today the question is also asked whether all development can be viewed quite so positively.

Those theologians who followed Newman and the modernists into the twentieth century in their concern with development have pursued this issue: Once development is accepted, *by what process* can one account for a substantial identity between what Loisy refers to as the basic Christian facts and their later interpretation?

Coming to the problem thirty years after the modernist condemnations, Rahner built on their work, avoided some of the pitfalls into which they had stumbled, and was more aware of the dimensions and complexity of the problem. There are two rather clear phases in his development writings. His early articles on development written in the 1950s and early 1960s expose his initial thinking on the subject. The later articles, beginning with some of the articles on Vatican II, begin to show an increasing sensitivity to history, to ecumenism and to contemporary philosophical and theological pluralism. These articles indicate a progression in Rahner's thinking on development leading to an increased emphasis on the hermeneutical task of the church. In the later works he suggests that the historical moment has come for the church to refocus and reinterpret its central mysteries rather than to develop the tradition any further in ongoing explicitation of individual doctrines.

The Early Articles on Development

Two articles, "The Development of Dogma" from 1954 and "Considerations on the Development of Dogma" from 1958[6] represent Rahner's earliest systematic reflections on the theory of development of dogma. Both reflect the caution toward the question characteristic of the post-modernist milieu in which they were written, but they succeed at the same time in advancing the discussion considerably beyond the limitations within which it had been operating during that time.

It is characteristic of Rahner's method that he tries to advance the discussion while retaining the positive elements of past approaches. Because of this methodology it is important to study these two early articles carefully, for Rahner sets forth there some principles of development that he never repudiates. Although his emphases increasingly lean in one direction rather than another, much of what he sets forth in these early articles remains as presupposition for his later writings in this area.

What characterized the state of theological thinking on development in the period that provided the proximate background and context for these articles? Nicholas Lash says that the concept of " 'homogeneous evolution' eventually came to mark the limits within which (so it was supposed) any orthodox discussion of doctrinal development must take place.''[7] This led to an exclusively positive and progressive theory of development not allowing for any change of direction or revolution. Lash notes that theologians basically sought to describe this evolution in one of two ways: through logical theories or through theological theories.[8]

Logical theories attempted to demonstrate how truths of faith could be logically derived from earlier propositions syllogistically. Theological theories emphasized "the unpredictability of historical process . . . . [In these theories] the ultimate ground of doctrinal development is the Spirit of God, and not merely the mind of man.''[9] The danger of an extreme application of this theological approach, of course, is a loss of a sense of history. It could result in a belief that whatever is proposed by the magisterium for belief at a certain period, under the guidance of the Holy Spirit, automatically constitutes authentic development. Lash suggests that it was this second approach to development which provided the proximate background for the 1950 definition of the assumption since this dogma was not easily accounted for by the prevailing logical theories.

Relocating the Starting Point: The 1954 Article

The definition of the assumption was the immediate provocation for Rahner's 1954 article on development of dogma. In this article he obviously is in dialogue with previous approaches, i.e., with the presuppositions of homogeneous evolution and logical and theological theories of development. The dogma of the assumption presented a clear problem to prevailing Catholic theories of development. How could a doctrine which so obviously appeared to be a "new truth" be perceived to be part of the "old truth"? The prevailing logical theories of development were unable to account for the emergence of such a doctrine. How could this doctrine be legitimated without resorting to purely supernatural or juridical approaches?

In the 1954 article, Rahner attempts to demonstrate that the logical theory of development, while having a certain validity, is inadequate alone to describe the process of development. He offers an alternative approach which still makes it possible to understand the evolution of a dogma such as the assumption as legitimate in a rational and historical way. The considerations and conclusions of this early article, although somewhat limited because of the particular focus of the article on the dogma of the assumption, nevertheless significantly move the discussion beyond its previous boundaries and point in the direction of Rahner's later thought.

In the early article he establishes some assumptions within

which, he says, the Roman Catholic discussion should proceed. First, there is dogmatic development and necessarily so. Second, the laws of dogmatic development can only be observed retrospectively. It is through investigation into the history of dogma that the laws of dogmatic development may be discovered. It was a mistake of past theories to think that there existed some *a priori* formal law that could be applied to all cases. Third, he reiterates his position on the truth claim of dogmatic statements. A proposition once it has been recognized as true by the church can never be considered false. "What the Church has once taken possession of as a portion of the Revelation which has fallen to her share, as the object of her unconditional faith, is from then on her permanently valid possession."[10]

Nevertheless, he says, there can be real change and development in dogma because a finite mind attempting to comprehend infinite truth will never grasp the whole all at one time. The formulations and conceptualizations of that truth can and must change according to changing historical situations. To say a proposition is inadequate, however, is in no way to admit that it is false, even partially: "Every formula in which the faith is expressed can in principle be surpassed while still retaining its truth."[11] Different aspects of truth become clear in response to the different needs of each historical period.

Within this framework, however, in his analysis of the nature of dogmatic development, Rahner moves the discussion considerably beyond its previous limits. Previous theories had presupposed that the starting point for dogmatic development was always a proposition and that such development could be accounted for by observing the logical progression of one proposition from another in syllogistic fashion. Rahner suggests that the history of dogmas illustrates that such a theory of itself is inadequate. There are dogmas for which such an explanation is not logically compelling.

He seeks another solution by shifting the understanding of the starting point for dogmatic development from proposition to event or experience. The closure of revelation, he says, far from meaning that the church has been left with a lifeless body of propositions to preserve, "a deposit," in fact means that it has been left in possession of the actual and definitive event of history from which it continues to live. "*Now* there is nothing more to come: no new age, no other aion, no fresh plan of salvation, but only the unveiling of what is already 'here' as God's presence at the end of a human time stretched out to breaking point . . . . [Revelation is] closed, because open to the concealed presence of the divine plenitude in Christ."[12] Because of the definitive and climactic nature of the Christ-event, the church always remains in possession of the reality from which it lives. This has radical significance for Rahner's understanding of dogma. Doctrinal development is not primarily a linear progression from proposition to proposition in which all the logical consequences of each proposition are gradually explicitated. It is rather "a reflexion on the propositions heard in living contact with the thing itself."[13]

As in the experience of love, in which the person first experiences love globally and then falteringly tries to articulate it, the church has received from the apostles not just propositions about their experience of Jesus, but that experience itself. Just as love grows through the always inadequate attempts to articulate it, the church grows in its self-understanding through ongoing reflection on the original experience from which it lives, as well as through reflection on the propositions in which that experience has been articulated. Thus dogmatic development can involve the development of new articulations of faith from the church's ongoing reflection on its original experience of the event of revelation. Such development is legitimate since the new proposition's connection to the already possessed experience can be demonstrated rationally, unlike the purely theological or super-natural theories. "The objective connexion between the new proposition and the old knowledge is not merely that between something logically explicit and something logically implicit in two propositions; it is rather a connexion between what becomes partially explicit in a proposition and the unreflexive, total spiritual possession of the entire *res,* so that this explicit proposition is at the same time more and less than its implicit source."[14] This explanation of the connection introduces a new possibility into the previous discussion. No longer are the alternatives either to accept totally new propositions of faith or to accept as dogma only propositions formally or virtually derived from previous propositions, but "a third possibility is open and that is a development and unfolding of the original treasures of faith under a positive influence of the light of faith bestowed upon the Church."[15]

Two important consequences follow from this early contribution to the development discussion. First, because of the complex and historical nature of the development of dogma more than one method of explication will be required. Purely rational methods will continue to have their place, but, he says, it would be theological naturalism to rely on such methods to explain completely all doctrinal development. Dogmatic development can be understood as starting from a pre-thematic possession of the whole reality rather than from propositions. This insight has important implications for the unfolding of Rahner's later thought on development.

Second, Rahner says that these new approaches indicate the possibility that one can have certainty in faith with regard to doctrinal development even if logical explanations are not completely compelling. "A *sure* knowledge is acquired in the form of knowledge in *faith* proper to the *Church* as such (if she steps in) not just through the merely logical explication of propositions as such but through the luminous power of the Spirit in contact with the *res* itself.''[16] Thus Rahner offers an approach to development which does not rely purely on either supernatural, juridical or logical motives for belief.

Rahner's earliest foray into the theory of development of dogma, then, is very much conditioned by the problems raised for Roman Catholic theology by the definition of the assumption. He is primarily concerned to relocate the starting point for development in the original global experience of revelation which is already possessed by the church rather than in original propositions. This, he says, offers wider possibilities for the assessment of the legitimacy of all such development.

Elements in Dogmatic Development: The 1958 Article

In this article Rahner again attempts to widen the discussion by pointing out the variety of factors which must be considered in working out an adequate theory of development. Those elements which Rahner sees as essential to any analysis of dogmatic development are: 1. Spirit and grace; 2. the magisterium; 3. concept and word; 4. tradition; 5. the acknowledged presence of dogma as dogma, revealed by God.[17]

The first three elements reiterate material already mentioned in this and previous chapters. In the areas of tradition and the process of dogma's coming to be acknowledged as dogma, however, Rahner significantly advances the state of the question.

Tradition. Rahner defines tradition as ''the process of 'being handed on.'''[18] This process begins with the fact that with any type of communication there is always a speaker and a hearer. Thus by the very fact of being heard — of being assimilated by the mind of the hearer — what is communicated undergoes a development. Is this traditioning process necessarily progressive and linear, leading to always greater articulation of the original revelation?

Based on his metaphysics of knowledge, Rahner sees development as *two*-directional. Individual propositions of faith are grasped under the unified *a priori* of the light of faith. This leads, on the one hand, to an ever increasing articulation of that fullness which is grasped in the light of faith but is only ever inadequately articulated. On the other hand, however, since all propositions are experienced in contact with the original experience, this results in a dynamism of return into the mystery of that infinite horizon. Thus he says dogmatic development is expansive in one direction and simplifying in the other. "It is not at all as if dogmatic development must always move in the direction of multiplying individual assertions. Just as important, indeed, strictly speaking still more important, is the development in the line of simplification, toward an ever clearer view of what is really intended, towards the single mystery, an intensification of the experience in faith of what is infinitely simple and in a very essential sense obvious."[19]

It is significant that Rahner calls attention to this insight so early in his writing on development of dogma. It is an insight that becomes increasingly important in his later Vatican II and post-Vatican II thought on development. But it is not only in those later writings that this aspect of dogmatic development becomes important. Already in 1957 he suspects that it is the second dynamism which should be becoming increasingly significant in the church's life. "Theology today might well take up more intensively the other charge that falls to it, and in practice, to it alone: the reduction of the multiplicity of faith's assertions to their ultimate structures, in the intelligence of which under certain circumstances the all-embracing and overwhelming mystery of God is more powerfully present for us today than where the spirit only enlarges upon the variety of the individual assertions and further distinctions among them.''[20] With the catalyst of Vatican II, Rahner focuses more and more on the significance and necessity of this second dynamism, the dynamism of return into mystery.

The recognition of dogma as dogma. The second major area in which Rahner offers clarifications helpful to a fuller understanding of the process of dogmatic development concerns the question of how a truth which has for a long time been more or less consciously in the church's mind comes to be recognized explicitly as dogma. He defines dogma in its fullest sense as follows: ''Where a dogma is present to the full extent of its being, it implies that the conscious faith of the Church, definitively instructed by the magisterium of the Church, holds it *as* revealed by God.''[21] The question is how this recognition of a truth as revealed comes to be. Again he says that it cannot be merely through the affirmation and external imposition by the pope or magisterium. This is so because unless the magisterium were to declare a totally new revelation (which is impossible), it is in fact basically recognizing something that was already there, and the question remains: How does this recognition take place? ''How and on what grounds and with what right does the believing mind of the Church take the step from a stage in which it possessed a truth without having *consciously* recognized it as revealed by God, to the stage of making such an assertion?''[22]

At this stage in his writings Rahner sees this as the key question of dogmatic development. ''By what *right*, consciously known and demonstrable, does the transition take place from the stage in which a proposition is not yet held as certainly revealed by God to the stage where it is accepted as certainly revealed by God?''[23] Logical proofs are not sufficient to account for this transition and the assent of faith which it requires. For his solution, Rahner turns to the traditional understanding of the *analysis fidei.* The church's coming to recognize a dogma is parallel to an individual's coming to faith for the first time. Although the rational presuppositions for coming to faith are involved in the process and essential to it, they do not account for the whole process. Faith is not irrational, but neither does it rest entirely on rational premises.

Thus there is a "leap of faith" involved both in coming to faith and, analogously, in the church's recognition of "new" dogma. In fact, what is involved in dogmatic development is the church, as a whole, coming to faith. Explicit promulgation by pope and magisterium only follows the collective coming to faith of the *whole* church. "The faith of the Church with regard to a revealed truth as such intervenes prior to the act of the extraordinary magisterium, and hence (in connexion with the ordinary magisterium) in the form of an almost imperceptible growth and ripening of this specified consciousness of the faith, as it 'comes to itself.' "[24] What is the function of the pope and the magisterium in recognizing dogma then if the faith of the church comes to consciousness in the *whole* church which involves both magisterium and people? Rahner does not envision a split between the two. "The Pope is the point at which the collective consciousness of the whole Church attains effective self-awareness, in a manner which is authoritative for the individual members of the Church."[25] The pope can act as articulator for the whole believing church community, of the dogma which has come to consciousness in its midst.

Rahner considers the issues he has dealt with in the two early articles on development as preliminary to engaging more fully in a discussion of dogmatic development. They move the discussion beyond the limitations of the post-modernist approach and open the way for the more far-reaching ideas of Rahner's Vatican II and post-Vatican II work.

Other Early Articles

Articles dealing with various individual dogmas also provide some illustration of Rahner's earlier views on development. The assumption and the immaculate conception are the subjects of numerous articles. Some other dogmas which he investigates around this time are those related to indulgences, the resurrection of the body, the virgin birth, the sacrament of penance, and of course articles on aspects of christology, beginning with his famous article, "Current Questions in Christology." In this article he makes his famous observation that a defined dogma should be regarded not as the end to development, but as the beginning.[26] One of Rahner's preoccupations in these articles is with what he observes to be a "shrinking" process which has happened concomitantly with the expansion of dogmas through the centuries (with penance and christology, for example). In the case of penance, he says, our understanding and acceptance of the doctrine could be considerably enriched by a recalling of certain elements which at one time were an important part of the church's understanding and now have fallen into disuse. Thus he says the church's development of dogma is not totally positive and cumulative. As different dimensions of a dogma become emphasized, others are "forgotten."

He also notes that whole dogmas sometimes fall by the wayside in such fashion. So development of dogma in one sense is cumulative, but in another sense certain truths lose their existential impact in the lives of Christians, and, therefore, seem to be lost to the church. In these early articles he speaks against what he sees as the reduction of Christian faith to short formulas which might eliminate the need for grappling with these difficult doctrines. "The works of God are in fact too rich in their reality to allow these riches to be rendered adequately by a short formula, no matter how clear and powerful the latter may be."[27] This points to a significant shift since Rahner later endorses short formulas as the best approach to present the faith in the contemporary world.

Dogmas can lose their existential impact, he says, in addition to the process of shrinking, by a process of accretion. This is what happened with the doctrine of the virgin birth. As the doctrine developed through history certain concrete details were added which were popularly supposed to belong to the essence of the doctrine. The actual affirmation about the virgin birth which can be established as relating to the apostolic deposit is, however, very limited. "Church doctrine affirms with the real substance of tradition, that Mary's childbirth, as regards both child and mother, like the conception, is, in its total reality, as the completely human act of this 'virgin', in itself. . . an act corresponding to the nature of this mother, and hence it is unique, miraculous and 'virginal.' "[28] This, he says, absolves modern people from the obligation to believe some of the later additions to the basic tradition which have been stumbling blocks to faith.

At this early stage, then, Rahner is concerned to rehabilitate those dogmas that have lost their existential significance through a process either of shrinkage or of accumulation of related affirmations which do not belong to the true dogma. These articles point, on the one hand, to Rahner's basic conviction that dogmas, once they have explicitly come into the church's consciousness, are irrevocable. On the other hand, he says, dogmatic development is not a simple unilinear progression; essential things can be forgotten and non-essential things can be added. At this early stage Rahner is occupied with defending dogma as it has developed in the church and with demonstrating the legitimacy of that development albeit in terms that go considerably beyond previous theories.

Probably the clearest example of Rahner's approach in this period is found in his early article, "Current Problems in

Christology."[29] In christology too Rahner is concerned that truths have been "forgotten" which if restored could move christology beyond the monophysite, mythological understandings which had so often characterized popular belief. He proposes to show "by means of a kind of transcendental hermeneutics *starting from dogma* [my italics]"[30] that the church's dogma, although true, does not exhaust the biblical testimony and thus leaves room for further development. In this article, as in the others we have mentioned, Rahner starts from the actual dogma. He does not try to demonstrate any logical progression starting with the data of scripture. This article reiterates the permanence and truth of the dogma itself but at the same time recognizes the need for formulations of that truth to be surpassed. "Anyone who takes seriously the 'historicity' of human truth (in which God's truth too has become incarnate in Revelation) must see that neither the abandonment of a formula nor its preservation in petrified form does justice to human understanding."[31]

Rahner too refers in this article, at least in an oblique way, to the global certainty that precedes the church's articulation of dogma. "For it is the bitter grief of theology and its blessed task too, always to have to seek (because it does not clearly have present to it at the time) what, in a true sense —in its historical memory — it has always known."[32] He deals mostly, however, with an attempt to break open the Chalcedonian formula as a beginning point for further development.

These articles about individual dogmas in most cases deal primarily with the problem of opening up the dogmas so they can be understood and lived by people today. Chapter 4 will say more about this. The mention of formal aspects of development is for the most part only incidental. Insofar as they do this, they reflect the theology of the early development articles, perhaps the more traditional aspects of those articles in many cases. He is at pains to show that these dogmas can be related to the "apostolic

deposit'' but that their development has often involved thought
processes beyond the purely formal explicitation of one revealed
statement from another.

This was Rahner's method of dealing with dogmatic development in the period prior to Vatican II. There has been a
legitimate process of development of dogma in the church which
includes all the elements which have been outlined above. It is
important to understand this process correctly to avoid the
misconceptions to which it has been subject on all sides in the
past. Essentially in these early writings Rahner understands the
process as evolutionary or organic with the important nuances
which have been mentioned above. As outlined in the early
articles this is a process that could continue in the same form
although as has been noted Rahner entertains the suspicion that
it may not. This is clearly a transitional approach, embodying
some aspects from earlier discussions and at the same time
sending out tentative feelers in new directions. A catalyst was
needed to solidify the direction of his thought. That catalyst was
Vatican II.

Vatican II — New Perspectives

Rahner was among the theologians such as Congar and de
Lubac whose work in the decades prior to Vatican II had a
profound effect on the direction of Vatican Council II. The
council, in turn, however, also had a profound effect on Rahner.
It opened doors and let in fresh air to a degree even he had not
dared to hope. Rahner's assessment of the impact of the council
sets the stage for an understanding of the influence that the trends
he saw emerging from the council had on his understanding of
dogma and its development.

Immediately prior to the council, Rahner's biggest hopes

seem to have been for inner church renewal, primarily clarification of certain ecclesial structures. He discusses, for example, collegiality, the relationship of primacy and episcopacy, the relationship of hierarchy to people of God. He also looks for some changes in church discipline, ''questions such as those concerning the restoration of the diaconate in keeping with the times, questions of adapting the laws of the Eucharistic fast and of fasting and abstinence in general to life as it is today.''[33] Although before the council Rahner had expressed cautious optimism about these reforms in church structures and discipline, he remained very pessimistic about any reform in the area of doctrine. ''Theology and the average proclamation from our pulpits and in the schools being what they are, it cannot seriously be expected. . .that there will be any essential difference in the Council's theological decrees from what is true of present-day theology in the schools, in the pulpit and in theological books.''[34] Rahner even expressed some fear that the council would feel compelled to make new dogmatic definitions in controversial areas.[35] Much to his surprise, however, the charismatic element in the church penetrated its official workings and produced a council with ramifications far beyond what Rahner, or others, had expected.

In the immediately post-conciliar writings there begins to be a cautious shift in his assessment of its significance. Exceeding Rahner's expectations the council had touched areas of church life far beyond mere structural or disciplinary change. In an article called ''The Changing Church'' written in 1965, Rahner responds to those who ''have the impression that people are discussing anything and everything, questioning everything, that everything is collapsing, that their own perhaps hard-earned and dearly-bought rigid adherence to the doctrine, and above all to the traditional practice, of the Church. . .is disavowed and almost despised by the Church and its leading representatives.''[36]

Obviously far more had happened than the innocuous changes Rahner had predicted! In response to this confusion this article attempts to clarify the difference between "ecclesiastically binding and, in the strictest case, dogmatically defined teaching of the Church on the one hand, and Church law and the actual living practice of the Church on the other."[37] This was pastorally necessary because much popular Catholic teaching of the time had blurred this distinction, leaving the faithful with the impression that all of church teaching and law was divine revelation and therefore unchangeable.

But Rahner also points out a changeable element within the dogma of the church itself. Although he reiterates his early contention that dogma once declared is irrevocable, he clarifies this by saying, "It cannot change back, it cannot be abolished (like a positive ecclesiastical law). But it can change forward in the direction of the fullness of its own meaning and unity with the one faith in its totality and its ultimate grounds."[38] This is not a new idea for Rahner. It can be found in the earlier development articles. Perhaps the biggest difference in this article from the earlier ones is its pastoral tone. It is less technical, and addressed to a non-specialist audience. With the Vatican Council, ideas that Rahner had only been able to advance tentatively within professional theological circles entered into the mainstream of Catholic life. What are some of the themes that emerged from the council which had significant effects on his thinking on doctrinal development?

First, where the earlier articles were exclusively focused on Roman Catholics, Rahner now sees that one of the most compelling reasons calling for new formulations of dogma is the situation of ecumenical dialogue. Roman Catholics must be able to talk a language that other Christians can understand.[39] Because of Vatican II's new attitude of openness to the modern world, not only must Roman Catholics be able to talk to other Christians but they must also be able to understand their faith in the contemporary cultural, sociological and philosophical milieu in which they exist.[40]

This is a theme that, once sounded here in these very early post-conciliar writings, occurs over and over again. Contemporary religious and philosophical pluralism has significantly altered the context in which today's religious beliefs must be articulated. No longer can Roman Catholics merely talk to one another in a scholastic terminology comprehensible to initiates alone. During this period he wrote articles entitled "Ideology and Christianity," "Reflections on Dialogue within a Pluralistic Society," "A Small Question Regarding the Contemporary Pluralism in the Intellectual Situation of Catholics and the Church," "Marxist Utopia and the Christian Future of Man," and "The Man of Today and Religion."[41] All these indicate Rahner's growing awareness that, since Vatican II's open doors, the church's understanding of its faith must take place within the context of the pluralistic world in which Christians now live.

These articles also evidence Rahner's recognition that after the council philosphy will no longer be the only partner in the understanding of Christian faith but that faith today will also be impacted by, and must be understood in relationship to, the social and natural sciences. As well, the church's explicit recognition of the positive values in this pluralistic world leads Rahner to emphasize one element of his understanding of dogma much more forcefully than he had in the earlier articles. Since the situation of pluralism implies that humankind will speak many languages, philosophical, sociological, psychological, not all comprehensible one to the other, Rahner suggests that the time is over for an ever increasing explicitation and development of the church's dogma in the one language of scholastic philosophy. Rather, he says:

It is conceivable that genuine 'progress' in dogmatic development in the future will move, not so much in the direction of a wider, more exact unfolding and precise definition of traditional dogma, but simply in that of a more living, radical grasp and statement of the ultimate fundamental dogmas themselves. A unified, universally valid statement of this kind could be accompanied by quite a number of theologies juxtaposed in a pluralist way, not contradicting each other of course, but not susceptible of being positively incorporated into a higher synthesis.[42]

This is not a new idea for Rahner, but the experience of Vatican II seems to convince him that now is the time for this second movement of dogma, the return into mystery, to become the focal point for the analysis and development of dogma. He returns to this theme over and over again in his later writings, developing it more fully and exploring its implications.

This new situation in the church of the future, Rahner says, will be brought about partially by its growing diaspora situation. No longer will Christianity be the religion of nations into which large numbers of people are born. He envisions the post-conciliar church as more and more a "little flock" of those who consciously join it and exercise a sign function in relation to the rest of the world. The world he sees as having become smaller and smaller due to increasing communications technology. Thus, he says, one of the unique things about today's world is that while there were always different cultures and philosophical languages, etc., it was not always so necessary or even possible for these different groups to interact with each other. In today's world people can no longer carry on their own intra-group discussions oblivious to other philosophical and sociological complexes. This situation exists both within the church, which Rahner points out is now no longer a predominantly western European church, and in the church's dialogue with the rest of the world to which it is called to be a sign.[43]

One might summarize this very brief account of Rahner's early reflections on the impact of Vatican II by saying that as a result of Vatican II and its opening the doors to the modern world, Rahner realized that Catholic theology can no longer be done in a purely inner church fashion. From the time of Vatican II on, Rahner's theology is done much more in contact with both secular and religious elements of the contemporary world. He takes more seriously, or at least more concretely, the impact of the historical epoch in which the church is living as a significant influence upon its theology and life.

Rahner views Vatican II as the beginning of a new era in the church, not as a conclusion. He warns against a tendency merely to exegete and expound the decrees of the council and bind the church forever to its formulations. Rather Rahner sees in the council a dynamism leading beyond its own stage, which was limited by the state of theology it grew out of, as was Rahner's own earlier theology, and into a new vision of the church.

These developments at Vatican II lead Rahner in his somewhat later writings to develop two key ideas which affect his thinking on dogma: 1. Vatican II as indicative of a real caesura in the church's history leading into a new period of its history, and 2. the new period as the era of a pluralistic world church. These ideas have important implications for his understanding of the future role of dogma.

Development of Dogma in a World-Church

Rahner saw Vatican II as the inauguration of the new era of the world-church. The world-church is a church no longer confined to western European culture and values, a church which no longer exists in other cultures as an exporter of the western values it had epitomized. For Rahner, the world-church is a church which grows out of the various cultures and values in which it exists, i.e., Asian, African, Latin American. It is also a church in dialogue with the secular cultures in which it lives as a small minority.

This transition to the world-church is something like a "qualitative leap" in the church's self-understanding.[44] Vatican II thus marks a major caesura in the history of the church, only the second such caesura in this history. Each of these two points, Rahner says, involved a significant change in the church's self-understanding and the setting of a new direction. There are three major epochs divided by the two caesurae as follows: "1. The short period of Judeo-Christianity; 2. The period of the Church in a particular cultural group, that of Hellenism and European culture and civilization; 3. The period in which the Church's living space is from the very outset the whole world."[45]

Rahner's thesis that we have arrived at this third moment or phase in the church has important consequences for his understanding of development of dogma. In this new phase of the church dogma must function differently. In a 1977 article, Rahner parallels the post-Vatican II church situation to that of the early church which came into existence in a non-Christian and often hostile spiritual and cultural environment. The long middle period by contrast, beginning roughly after the third century, he says, was characterized by a generally homogeneous world view. This environment provided the context for an increasing differentiation of the substance of faith into more and more detailed individual elements. This was the period of the Summa, catechisms, and Denzinger-theology. "It was the time when lengthy papal encyclicals dealing with comparatively detailed questions of Christian faith could be taken as a matter of course; when the magisterium reacted meticulously and swiftly to real or supposed infringements of particular teachings from this detailed system.''[46]

Today, Rahner says, as in its early days, the church finds itself in a new diaspora situation in a secular world. Once again as in the early church it must work out its understanding of belief in an often unsympathetic non-Christian world. Increasing pluralism within the church as well as without could cause the history of the church of the future and its doctrine to be as conflictual as the great periods of dogmatic dispute in the church's early centuries. In a church that takes the world *as world* seriously, doctrinal development must take place both in confrontation with and in positive relationship to that world. In this situation the approach to dogmatic development characteristic of the more homogeneous second period is no longer appropriate and a new mode of developing and reunderstanding faith must be found.

> We have undoubtedly entered into a new phase of the history of faith and thus also of the history of dogma and theology. It is a question today no longer of an increasingly detailed explication of the basic substance of faith within a homogeneous milieu, with its own common horizons of understanding; on the contrary, it is a question of acquiring a new understanding (while preserving, of course, the traditional substance of faith) of the faith as one and whole in a non-Christian milieu, in a new period of a global world civilisation into which new world cultures which were never Christian have entered.[47]

The Confrontation with History

In the later writings Rahner does not attempt to analyze dogma in terms of its internal processes and forces of propulsion, but sees it always in relationship to the history, both religious and secular, out of which it grows. He understands dogma much more explicitly as growing out of the different cultural epochs from which it arises. "The actual history of dogma took place, therefore, not in the style of a purely logical continuity of statement and explanation, but in the perpetual interaction of sacred and secular history, history of faith and of thought, which cannot wholly be displayed in theoretical form."[48] This is quite a different approach to the analysis of dogma's development from the earliest articles cited in this chapter.

Rahner sees overall two major movements characterizing the church's development through the centuries and sees these movements reflected in the development of dogma. The first great epoch of dogma participated in the gradual unfolding of the church's understanding of God's revelation in terms of the relatively "local" environments in which it found itself, Judaism, Hellenism, and the west.

Gradually the church's faith needs to be detached from these limited world views to enable it as a unity to engage truly in dialogue with the whole world. This second phase of development has been inaugurated by Vatican II. The idea of the two phases in dogmatic development is not new to Rahner. It had already appeared in his early 1950s articles where he described dogma as having both an expansive moment and a moment of return into mystery. There, however, the paradigm grew primarily out of his metaphysics of human knowing. Here he sees it as reflecting actual historical development.

What will characterize dogma in this new situation of dialogue with the world? Many of Rahner's articles written in the 1970s focus on the new emphases in dogma which he sees as necessary for the world-church.

The Impact of Pluralism

As mentioned above, because of the pluralism characteristic of the contemporary world Rahner sees an end to the proliferation of dogmas in increasingly marginal areas of faith. Instead he sees the need for a concentration on and reformulation of the most central mysteries of faith in languages comprehensible to the different groups making up the church. The task then becomes the hermeneutical task of reunderstanding and reinterpreting the basic core of Christian faith in such a way that it can be understood in the multiform environment in which it exists. What Rahner advocates for the future is a mystical theology, with an emphasis clearly on the second movement in dogmatic development, the return to contemplation of the central mysteries of faith, which he envisioned even in his early articles.

The Role of Theology

Because Rahner, in these later works, does not see further actual development of dogma in the formal sense, theology takes on increasing importance in his view of the future. The enormous pluralism in the world, he says, requires that the central mysteries of faith be articulated by different theologies which may in fact seem to be irreconcilable with each other. "These differences will be so great that as theologies it will be quite impossible for them to be covered by, or subsumed under any one single homogeneous theology."[49] Although there must continue to be dialogue among the different theologies the pluralism in outlook will be

too great to allow any one theology to emerge as *the* theology
of the church as scholastic theology did in the past. ''There will
no longer be any one theology of the Church. Rather there will
be theologies of the Church in the plural, each of them having
a different bearing upon and approach to the one creed.''[50]

Since there is no longer a homogeneity of world view and
language, it is impossible to foresee a further homogeneous, evolutionary unfolding of the doctrines which would be intelligible
to and binding on the whole church. Theology in its own right,
then, in the future will attain increasing importance since its work
will no longer be seen as primarily the preparatory tentative
groundwork toward the new definition of a dogma. Among the
many modes of articulation of God's revelation which were noted
in Chapter 2, scripture, creeds, dogmatic statements, and
theological statements, Rahner sees theology as the most
appropriate mode of formulation for the present pluralistic world.
If faith is to be expressed in divergent theologies, however, will
this not result in the loss of the unity of the church's faith, which
has been preserved in creeds and dogmatic statements, binding
on all?

The Creed and the Unity of Faith

Rahner suggests that the unity of faith can be safeguarded
in two ways. On the propositional or categorical level, Rahner
sees the ancient creeds and early doctrinal decisions of the church
continuing to function as touchstones for unity. The various
theologies and short contemporary creeds can be tested for
orthodoxy by being asked if they are attempts to describe the
same reality that the early creeds and doctrinal definitions were
describing. Thus Rahner does see the early creeds and definitions
retaining a function in the church, as starting points for today's

understandings. However, he says, it would be a misunderstanding to think that reciting the old creeds or formulas in the philosophical and theological language in which they were written would be an adequate faith form for today.

Rahner, then, expects the tradition to continue to develop but not through new dogmatic statements in the narrow sense. Rather it will develop through the increasingly pluralistic articulation of various theologies all united through their common relation to the early creeds and doctrinal statements of the church. It is interesting that Rahner locates the norm for development not only in scripture but in the early formulations of the church, i.e., the early definitions and creeds.

Rahner also sees a transcendental locus of unity in the church and reminds us that the unity of faith does not rest exclusively in its propositional formulations. As was discussed in some detail in Chapter 1, Rahner understands propositions as an intrinsic element in the exposition of faith which bring one into contact with the very reality they articulate. Thus there is a deeper unity of faith in the church because the church's formulations of faith both grow out of and lead back into that fundamental incomprehensible mystery which they attempt to express.

Finally Rahner sees Vatican II as a model and exemplar for the future in that it made no formal dogmatic definitions. "At least in *Gaudium et Spes* the Council adopted spontaneously a mode of expression which had the character neither of dogmatic teaching valid for all time nor of canonical enactments, but was perhaps to be understood as the expression of 'instructions' or 'appeals.' "[51]

This overview of Rahner's understanding of development of dogma reveals a significant progression in his thought. In the early works he attempts to provide a rationale for the past development of Christian doctrine, while in his later work he is more concerned with elaborating an understanding of the ongoing development of Christian faith suitable to a post-conciliar pluralistic world. This leads him to suggest that the time is past for a continuing differentiation of Christian faith into ever more specific and binding doctrines. The articulation of faith in this new historical situation will better be expressed in a diversity of short creeds and theological statements. The particular need of today's church is an increased hermeneutic effort to reunderstand and reinterpret the essentials of Christian faith within this new horizon of understanding. It is as a whole and as unified under the major dogmas of Christianity that faith can best be made living and active within today's secular world.

Notes

¹ "Theology in the New Testament," *TI* V: 26.

² "Considerations on the Development of Dogma," *TI* IV: 5.

³ There are a number of studies of the various theories of doctrinal development proposed since the time of Newman and the modernists. See Jan Walgrave, *Unfolding Revelation* (Philadelphia: Westminster, 1972), which contains both a history of the question and the author's own synthesis; Nicholas Lash, *Change in Focus* (London: Sheed and Ward, 1973); William E. Reiser, *What Are They Saying about Dogma?* (New York: Paulist, 1978); Herbert Hammans, "Recent Catholic Views on the Development of Dogma," in *Man as Man and Believer, Concilium* 21, ed. E. Schillebeeckx (New York: Paulist, 1967), pp. 53-63.

⁴ Newman's *An Essay on the Development of Christian Doctrine* was of course a seminal effort in this attempt to understand the fact and nature of development of doctrine. See John Henry Cardinal Newman, *An Essay on the Development of Christian Doctrine*, ed. Charles Frederick Harrold (New York: Longmans, Green and Co., 1949).

⁵ Alfred Loisy, *The Gospel and the Church* (Philadelphia: Fortress, 1976), pp. 149-150. This text is a reprint of the translation of Christopher Home which was published in 1903 by Isbister & Co., Ltd. in London and reprinted in 1912 by Charles Scribner's Sons in New York.

⁶ "The Development of Dogma," *TI* I: 39-77; "Considerations on the Development of Dogma," *TI* IV: 3-35.

⁷ Lash, p. 121.

⁸ Ibid., p. 123.

⁹ Ibid., p. 124.

¹⁰ "The Development of Dogma," *TI* I: 43.

¹¹ Ibid., p. 44.

[12] Ibid., p. 49.

[13] Ibid., p. 50.

[14] Ibid., p. 67.

[15] Ibid., p. 52.

[16] Ibid., pp. 52-53.

[17] "Considerations on the Development of Dogma," *TI* IV: 11-35.

[18] Ibid., p. 24.

[19] Ibid., p. 26.

[20] Ibid.

[21] Ibid., p. 27.

[22] Ibid., p. 28.

[23] Ibid., p. 29.

[24] Ibid., p. 32.

[25] Ibid., p. 34.

[26] "Current Problems in Christology," *TI* I: 149.

[27] "Forgotten Truths concerning the Sacrament of Penance," *TI* II, trans. Karl-H. Kruger (Baltimore: Helicon, 1963), p. 136.

[28] *"Virginitas in Partu,"* *TI* IV: 162.

[29] "Current Problems in Christology," *TI* I: 149-200.

[30] Ibid., p. 154.

[31] Ibid., p. 150.

[32] Ibid., p. 151.

[33] "On the Theology of the Council," *TI* V: 264-265.

[34] Ibid., p. 262.

[35] Ibid., p. 264.

[36] *The Christian of the Future,* trans. W.J. O'Hara (New York: Herder & Herder, 1967), p. 10.

[37] Ibid., p. 11.

[38] Ibid., p. 24.

[39] Ibid., p. 23.

[40] Ibid.

[41] "Ideology," pp. 43-58; "Reflections," pp. 31-42; "Intellec-

tual Situation," pp. 21-30; "Marxist Utopia," pp. 59-68; "Man of Today," pp. 3-20, in *TI* VI.

⁴² *Christian of the Future,* p. 34.

⁴³ Ibid., pp. 78-85.

⁴⁴ "Basic Theological Interpretation of the Second Vatican Council," *TI* XX: 80.

⁴⁵ Ibid., p. 83.

⁴⁶ "Yesterday's History of Dogma and Theology for Tomorrow," *TI* XVIII, trans. Edward Quinn (New York: Crossroad, 1983), p. 32. The above and following comments are also dependent on this article.

⁴⁷ Ibid., p. 33. See also *The Christian of the Future,* p. 99; "The Future of Theology," *TI* XI: 140; "Dream of the Future," *TI* XX: 139.

⁴⁸ Rahner, "Dogma," *ET:* 362.

⁴⁹ "The Future of Theology," *TI* XI: 139. See also "Pluralism in Theology," *TI* XI: 19.

⁵⁰ "The Future of Theology," *TI* XI: 139. See also "Pluralism in Theology," *TI* XI: 20.

⁵¹ "Theological Interpretation of Vatican II," *TI* XX: 89.

CHAPTER 4

Dogma and Christian Life

Dogma is legitimate not only theoretically but existentially insofar as it facilitates the Christian's entrance into the incomprehensible mystery which grounds human life. For Rahner, dogma is never an end in itself nor is assent to dogma on the basis of external authority. A major theme of his writings on dogma has been the existential relevance of the dogmas of Christian religion to Christian life in today's world. From an early focus on breaking open the many and variegated doctrines of faith (including those of less central significance) to show their relationship to contemporary Christian life, he moves to an emphasis more on showing the interrelatedness of the variety of dogmas under the three great dogmas of the Christian faith, Trinity, grace and incarnation, and on facilitating their existential impact. He gives the impression in his later writings that some of the more obscure doctrines of faith might well be suffered to fall into benign neglect in order to allow a more intensive focus on the central truths.

Phase I: Early Attempts To Demonstrate the Existential Relevance of Dogmas

In his early article, "The Immaculate Conception," Rahner attempts to show that the immaculate conception is a legitimate dogma over against those who question it as peripheral or not contained in scripture and to show that this doctrine is still relevant for Christian belief today. At this early stage he still advocates the continuing practical significance of the variety of existing dogmas. All the truths of faith should play an important part in the Christian's spiritual life. At the same time, Rahner's main justification for the dogma of the immaculate conception, for example, lies in its connection to the redemption. "Such a commemoration, rightly understood, is a celebration of the mystery of our Redemption and a praise of the grace of the one Lord in whose name alone there is salvation."[1] So, in fact, a spirituality of the immaculate conception is a spirituality focused on an essential truth of faith, redemption. Thus already in Rahner's early works there is the tendency to legitimize the various dogmas by demonstrating their connection to the central mysteries of faith.

His concern that dogma not only be legitimate but active in the lives of Christians is more clearly demonstrated by a slightly later article entitled "The Dogma of the Immaculate Conception in Our Spiritual Life." "But it would be heretical gnosticism, or the false assertion that truth and salvation, faith and love are simply the same, to maintain that this truth is told us *merely* because it is true. We can — indeed we must — ask ourselves, therefore, what a revealed truth means *for us* over and above the fact directly proclaimed by it."[2]

In this article Rahner points out that for the dogma of the immaculate conception to have existential significance for us we must see Mary's immaculate conception not as a unique instance — discontinuous with our own lives — but rather as directly connected to our own experience of salvation. "Our God willed to love one human being in that way, but in that love of his for Mary, encompassing her whole life with love from beginning to end, we too are implied."[3] Without the example of the immaculate conception, Rahner says, one might be tempted to view guilt and grace as co-determining and equal aspects of the structure of our human existence. The immaculate conception affirms the pre-eminence of grace over guilt, that God's yes, as Rahner calls grace, understood temporally as earlier in the case of the Virgin Mary, also encompasses our whole existence. There is Mary's way to perfection (preservation from guilt) and *our* way (forgiveness from guilt) — two complementary ways of understanding that our lives are from the beginning caught up in God's grace and that our salvation is only God's grace. Neither human guilt nor human good works are the sole constitutive components of that salvation.[4]

Rahner's articles on the immaculate conception illustrate well the approach to demonstrating the existential relevance of various dogmas to Christian life characteristic of Rahner's pre-conciliar writings. Numerous other articles utilize this same general approach.[5] He tries to break open the various dogmas to show that if human beings better understood themselves and the structures of their existence, and if they understood the various doctrines more accurately, not as they have often been misunderstood or distorted, they would see that the essential truths of the dogmas correspond to deep and central facets of existence.

In any number of these early articles Rahner refers to the "shrinking process," which has already been referred to in connection with his work on development of dogma.[6] He introduces "Remarks on the Theology of Indulgences" by commenting: "There are truths in the Church which, although they are not indeed disputed in their explicit (*'in thesi'*) formulation, are being silenced to death by the fact that no one takes any notice of them any longer in the practice of their religious life. They are to be found in the Catechism, but they are not inscribed 'in our hearts on tablets of flesh.' "[7] In these early works he is concerned to rehabilitate this wide variety of doctrines, so that they once again can occupy a place in the actual lives of Christians.

It is not enough, he says, that these doctrines be traditional and legitimately proclaimed in a formal way by the church, nor even that assent to these truths be demanded by the church. "They often cannot in any way be enjoined as a necessary part of men's lives — not even in the case of a member of the Church and not even by the threat of an anathema on such a member."[8] Clearly intellectual assent or assent based on external authority is insufficient. Obedience does not equal faith. Truths which remain only in the objective exterior catechism without entering into the "catechism of the heart" may remain true but they are no longer living. All these truths of faith must be brought into the "catechism of the heart" through the complementary analysis of both the content of the dogma and the structures of human existence aimed at showing their essential correlation. Rahner's approach to dogma, then, is essentially pastoral. Showing the objective legitimacy of a dogma is never enough: it must be proclaimed and explained in such a way as to show its existential significance for the life and spirituality of Christians. In these early writings Rahner is convinced that this task is possible. If we truly understand ourselves and understand the various dogmas aright we will discover their existential import and be able to integrate them into our Christian lives.

At this stage Rahner sees a grave danger that some of the traditional truths will be lost by those, both heretics and orthodox, who live only by the catechism of their own hearts. "We take cognizance of these truths and then push them (not on reflection, of course, but instinctively) to one side a little, to the periphery of thought and life, into the subconscious (as we would say nowadays), or into the sphere of the *fides implicita.*"[9] While never explicitly changing this conviction, Rahner's later writings imply that, because of the changed world, Christian life and spirituality in the future will probably need to allow some of the more peripheral beliefs to fall quietly by the wayside leaving Christian spirituality free to focus on the great and central mysteries of faith: grace, Trinity and incarnation. In fact, however, already in the early articles Rahner most often locates the claim to significance of the various dogmas in their interrelatedness to the great truths of faith. Thus his later work is more a development than a radical shift from his earlier work.

As was the case in his thinking on development, Vatican Council II seems to be the catalyst for a gradual shift from an emphasis on retrieving the manifold truths of the tradition to suggesting that in today's spirituality and the spirituality of the future, men and women may and should concentrate more on the essentials of faith and less on the more secondary doctrines.

In an article written in 1966, "Christian Living Formerly and Today," he suggests that today's Christian will "apply himself to the fundamental realities and truths of the Christian faith, and . . . count upon his *fides implicita* to cover many other secondary truths, derived from these, which he does not call in question."[10] The very doctrines that he suggests may become part of the *fides implicita* are those he was concerned with rehabilitating in his earlier articles: devotion to the Blessed Sacrament, veneration of the precious blood, the immaculate conception and indulgences, for example.[11] In this work he says that "our devotion must . . . be cut down to the bare essentials," in order "to enter upon a direct relationship with God in his ineffability."[12] In other words, he says that Christians must become mystics.

In the later writings the mystical tendency which is present all through Rahner's writings comes strongly to the fore. He becomes less and less concerned with the Christian's appropriation of a multiplicity of doctrines and more concerned that the Christian enter ever more profoundly into the contemplation of the central mystery of faith.

Phase II: The Vatican II and Post-Vatican Years

As mentioned in Chapter 3, immediately following Vatican II Rahner's writings begin to reflect much more awareness of the contemporary world and its problems, as well as a more explicit awareness of the ecumenical dimensions of all theological discussion. He seems to take more seriously than heretofore the fact that contemporary Roman Catholics no longer live in a narrow church-dominated world. For these Catholics, doctrines like the immaculate conception and indulgences may be more stumbling blocks than aids to faith. Therefore, one's pastoral approach to the contemporary Catholic must be different. It is far better, he argues, to focus on deepening the grasp and motivating power of the central doctrines which provide connections to other Christians and non-Christians than to dissipate energy by requiring explicit attention to more peripheral matters.

Rahner never suggests that these secondary doctrines are in error or should be repudiated, just that they may not function actively in the lives of many contemporary Christians. He becomes increasingly preoccupied with the actual world in which the post-Vatican II Christian lives his or her life and its impact on possibilities for belief.

Unifying the Dogmas

As Chapter 3 pointed out, Rahner sees in the present time the historical moment for a concentration on the second aspect of conceptualization or development, the return to the center. He therefore no longer emphasizes the need to meditate on the more peripheral dogmas in order to arrive through that meditation at the center of faith. Rather he emphasizes a more direct concentration on the central aspects of faith: Trinity, grace, incarnation and ultimately on contemplation of the holy mystery itself in silent awe. The Christian rather than ranging widely over the varieties of doctrines in the church is now called in his or her spiritual life to focus intensely in a more contemplative, mystical fashion at the transcendent core of his or her being. His changing attitude toward the Marian dogmas illustrates this later approach. Rahner recognizes that there had been an ongoing historical development in mariology culminating in the definition of the assumption in 1950. Although there had been some hope that this development would be continued with a new definition at Vatican Council II, the council rather set a new direction allowing a concentration on a unified Marian principle which sees Mary as intimately connected to the church. Rahner suggests that, following this direction, there will not be further quantitative expansion of the Marian dogmas, but rather that, "the old dogma will be both reconsidered and theologically assimilated under new aspects and against new backgrounds of understanding, which formerly were not so explicitly present."[13] This is a general paradigm for the future history of dogma as he envisions it.

What does this conviction indicate with regard to dogma? Is Rahner as committed to the role of dogma in religion as is popularly thought, or, if he was at one time, does he continue to be in his later works? Does the historical and cultural setting of Vatican II merely allow him to become more open about what in fact has been his position all along: that dogma is radically secondary and that religion is more properly concerned with that transcendent experience of the mystery of being common to all human beings? This is a question which Rahner's writings make it most difficult to answer. There is an ambiguity at the heart of Rahner's writings. On the one hand, he asserts strongly and often the importance of this historical/categorical dimension of experience. On the other hand, he seems most inclined personally to focus on the transcendental experience of mystery.

Three areas of Rahner's later theology help to illustrate how he views the necessity and significance of dogma in the actual lives of today's Christians: first, his views on foundational theology, especially as revealed in *Foundations of Christian Faith;* second, his work on faith or spirituality outside the church, i.e., the impact of "anonymous Christianity" on the centrality of dogma; finally, the role of dogma in the lives of those who are explicitly Christian.

A Foundational Theology for Today

Rahner's recognition of the need for a new foundational theology grew out of his teaching of seminarians and reflects a deep pastoral concern that Christian faith be apprehended not only as intellectually credible but also as spiritually fruitful. Rahner proposes that a better foundational theology, one which grasps the theology student spiritually and existentially as well as intellectually, would be one which focused on the transcendental conditions for the possibility of belief and on the few central mysteries of faith rather than on a multiplicity of propositions.

This is essentially the program he offers in his *Foundations of Christian Faith,* which he subtitles "An Introduction to the Idea of Christianity." In this important work Rahner tries to present Christianity, not as a collection of various propositions, but as a whole. It is a work intended to help the beginner come to a conscious and intellectually reasonable faith decision through scientific theological reflection on the essentials of Christianity.

The central mysteries of faith which are the subject matter of this introduction do not "consist in a rather large number of individual propositions which are unfortunately unintelligible.

The only really absolute mysteries are the self-communication of God in the depths of existence, called grace, and in history, called Jesus Christ, and this already includes the mystery of the Trinity in the economy of salvation and of the immanent Trinity. And this one mystery can be brought close to man if he understands himself as oriented towards the mystery which we call God.''[14] Abstracting from the many other issues which one might find in the catechism, or in older fundamental and dogmatic theology, Rahner presents for reflection this unified statement of what he considers the fundamentals of Christian faith. *Foundations* concentrates on making the "great" dogmas intelligible. It illustrates clearly that Rahner does not consider mere intellectual apprehension of even these essentials as sufficient, although *Foundations* is clearly oriented toward offering a rational grasp of Christianity. "For a Christian, his Christian existence is ultimately the totality of his existence. This totality opens out into the dark abysses of the wilderness which we call God . . . . The abyss of existence opens up in front of him. He knows that he has not thought enough, has not loved enough, and has not suffered enough.''[15] Obviously the way to faith is not primarily through intellectual apprehension of faith's content.

The approach and content of *Foundations* and statements such as the above raise the question again if for Rahner "falling into the abyss," the conscious experience of grace, is not the most fundamental meaning of religion and if the categorical mediation of that experience as reflected in dogmas and propositions, etc., is not really quite secondary. "Scientific theological reflection does not capture and cannot capture the whole of this reality which we realize in faith, hope, love, and prayer.''[16]

Rahner's work on the anonymous Christian specifies this question with particular intensity. If the rational content of faith, i.e., dogma, is central to Christianity, how can Rahner suggest that the majority of people will in fact be saved without explicit reference to this content?

Dogma and the Anonymous Christian

Rahner's theory of the anonymous Christian is sometimes misinterpreted to imply that because persons can be saved without any explicit contact with the content of the message of Christianity, that message and its ongoing mediation is rendered superfluous. For example, it has been suggested that the church's missionary effort would be unnecessary. Why preach the gospel to people who can be saved without it? Actually this is far from Rahner's intent. To critics of the theory of the anonymous Christian Rahner responds that he is trying to hold on to and balance two traditional church doctrines, ''outside the church there is no salvation'' and the universal saving will of God by pointing out that ''church'' is not necessarily co-extensive with its visible institutional boundaries. This is particularly critical today because in our enormous and diverse world there is a majority of people who will never come into contact with the Christian message, at least in any credible way. That the terminology of anonymous Christian might be inadequate or misleading Rahner accepts.

The theory of the anonymous Christian invokes the distinction between the ''original event of revelation consisting in the self-communication of God as addressed to all in virtue of his universal will to save and taking place at a preconceptual level in the roots of man's spiritual faculties on the one hand, and the objectification at the historical and conceptual level of this revelatory self-communication of God in that which we call revelation and the history of revelation in a more normal sense on the other.''[17] According to Rahner a true theological faith is present if a person accepts the pre-conceptual self-communication of God, even if this is not articulated in any explicitly religious way. "Whenever a man is true to the dictates of his conscience, whenever he does not reject an unconditional hope in the final moment of decision in spite of all disappointments and disasters in his experience of life, that is revelation. That is faith."[18] And that person is an anonymous Christian. But, he says, there is a dynamic by which this implicit faith strives to become explicit. He thus answers the critique of those who accuse him of rendering superfluous the conceptual content of Christianity. "This does not, however, mean that such explicit demonstrations of courageous hope, expressed in religious terms, are in any way superfluous or worthless."[19]

The church's missionary effort is not rendered unnecessary but is in fact aided by the theory of the anonymous Christian. The missionary does not preach "new" news but in fact helps the individual to illuminate and explicitate the experience of God which is already operating in the depths of his or her person. Rahner views contact with the dogmas and doctrine of the church as the fullness of that saving faith which is initiated in the transcendental depths of every person since every person, according to Rahner, stands under the offer of God's grace. Those who are confronted with the Christian message in a credible way become responsible for its content, i.e., a Christian who has a true understanding of faith cannot choose to live his or her life without reference to the explicit Christian message without being held culpable. Ultimate courage for life and systematic faith in Jesus Christ are fundamentally one and the same for a Christian.[20] Rahner does however point out that persons are not culpable for their failure to accept explicit Christianity unless they are presented with the message in a credible and clear way so that they are able to recognize it as the explicitation of their implicit faith.[21] The basic approach recounted above is characteristic of Rahner's articles concerned with anonymous Christianity. He asserts consistently that the concept of the anonymous Christian in no way intends to deprive the conceptual content of Christianity of its continuing importance.

There is a distinctive spirituality appropriate to those who come to salvation through implicit acceptance of the offer of God's grace as well as to those who are explicitly Christian. For Rahner that spirituality is foundational for all people which is "really animated by the innermost, free turning of man to God, which is sustained by God's grace."[22] The spirituality which grows out of church-relatedness is ultimately secondary. "At all events attachment to the Church must basically be judged only as a particular and, in the true sense, secondary element in piety. . . . There can be a saving piety which is not bound to the Church at all."[23] This piety which is outside the church is based on the experience which is the basic faith position of the anonymous Christian: implicit acceptance of God based on an acceptance of one's own transcendence. According to Rahner this is a true piety which is fundamental to both implicit and explicit Christians. It provides the depth dimension for church-related spirituality without which it can easily degenerate into mere extrinsicism. "The piety of the Church must always be clearly 'fed back' into that primal experience which is its basic material and which it interprets."[24] Church-related piety should be the fulfillment of that transcendental piety which is possible for all. But this is a fulfillment to which all are not called. "So incorporation in the Church is not the beginning but the end of the grace which, in its sovereign freedom, calls some people among others. These people form the Church, which is the historical sign of the victorious presence of God's grace in the world, and is. . .an actual, particular sign in human history of the fact that God is present through his grace in all piety."[25] The church is made up of those few called to explicit faith whose function is to be a sign of the salvation offered to all people of good will. Most people are saved by an unthematic giving over of themselves to the holy mystery. In a formulation which perhaps reflects the way many Catholics sometimes feel about the institutional church and its dogmas, Rahner says that to those who are called is given the additional burden of working out this salvation in the context of the church with its dogmas and doctrines.[26]

Realistically speaking, Rahner says, most of the world will be saved without contact with the dogma or doctrine of the church. Saving faith for such people may not be conceptualized or thematized in any specifically religious terms at all. Thus in his mind explicit acceptance of the dogma of the church cannot be absolutely constitutive for salvation. Although the movement toward conceptualization of transcendental experience of self and God (or the ability to recognize one's own experience in the formulations of the church) is the logical follow-through of transcendental experience, there are those who for many reasons either are unable to articulate that experience at all or if they are able to articulate it do not recognize it in the traditional doctrinal formulations of the church. These too are saved. Since one cannot be "more saved" or "less saved," fundamental acceptance of life in transcendental hope must be the only absolute requirement for salvation.

But the church *is* necessary for those who are called by God and given the grace to see their experience as fulfilled by the saving event of Jesus Christ and the church's subsequent reflection on that event.[27] Anyone so gifted who would choose to remain aloof from explicit articulation of faith in the church is culpable for that lack. Dogma is essential for salvation then for those called by God to be part of the visible church, those who are able to interpret this religious experience explicitly. The vast majority of humankind is saved through a more or less unthematic apprehension of God gained through trusting acceptance of their own existence. But what of explicit Christians? How constitutive is dogma even for those who consider themselves Christians and members of the church?

Dogma and the Ecclesial Christian

Rahner has much to say on this issue in his later writings. The impact of Vatican II plus his own contact with an increasingly secular and pluralistic world convinced him that the task which he had envisioned earlier, i.e., helping Christians to find in the many dogmas of the church not just abstract intellectual formulas but pointers to the incomprehensible mystery of God, may no longer be possible. Christians will live less and less by the printed catechism and more and more by the "catechism" of their own hearts. Rather than decrying this situation as he did earlier, Rahner attempts to deal pastorally with the reality of the church of today in which Christians no longer feel bound by the external imposition of dogmas, but rather pick and choose what seems helpful or meaningful for their living of Christian life.

A number of articles from Rahner's post-Vatican II period point to themes relevant for an understanding of the role he sees for dogma or doctrine in the Christian spirituality of the present and especially of the future. Rahner equates spirituality with "the problem of Christian living in the post-conciliar age."[28] This problem has individual, personal dimensions as well as social and political implications.

A first point to be considered in analyzing the role of dogma in today's spirituality is not new to his later period. Rahner is convinced that, important though the propositional content of faith may be, it is not ultimate. Persons do not come to faith primarily via a rational consideration of the dogmas (as was popularly thought in post-reformation Catholic theology) in which grace functioned to raise this natural process to the super-natural level in a fashion beyond human consciousness. This view sometimes led to identifying the life of faith with intellectual acceptance of the propositions of faith. Rahner, because of his understanding of grace, calls for a clear and definitive break with this school. That grace operates *within* human consciousness is a key element in the pervasive theology of grace which underlies Rahner's theology. And ultimately the assent of faith is not located primarily in a rational assent to the dogmas which is raised to the supernatural level, but in that transcendental experience of God in which the person accepts himself or herself and in doing so accepts God. This is the light of faith which illumines and makes relevant the dogmatic content of faith. Rahner is concerned that theology turn its attention to dealing with the "gap. . . between the grounds of credibility of Christian revelation and the actual decision to believe."[29] He finds the link in the traditional notion of the light of faith or grace of faith. Without this the dogmatic content of faith would remain purely external truths and the act of faith merely their external acceptance.

The Pastoral Problem

Rahner is convinced that because of lack of attention to this "depth dimension" many Christians have been imprisoned in a faith, based purely on obedience, that was often existentially meaningless. People must be helped to recognize and thematize the basic experience of mystery at the heart of their existence before they can be expected to find dogma meaningful and comprehensible. The primary act of faith for all people is a trustful acceptance of the mystery of life.

Rahner is concerned with the situation of those who experience faith in an impoverished way. The over-rationality of religion epitomized by the school of thought rejected by Rahner led to some Christians for whom faith was merely lifeless, lifelong adherence to externally imposed propositions. The pastoral task for today is to help people to recognize the experience of God which lies at the heart of all their existence, to accept that experience and thus to lay the groundwork for a proper appreciation of the categorcial content of faith as secondary to that experience though not superfluous.

> What is the situation, then, of ordinary Christians in their daily piety? They have at their disposal a large store of religious concepts, propositions, motivations and patterns of behaviour which all perform an important function in guiding their daily life and action. But in their day-to-day affairs they do not encounter with any clarity either the heart of their own subjectivity or God himself in his true self-communication. . . . How can this imprisonment in the objective and categorial reality of everyday existence, even religious, be broken?[30]

The problem is exacerbated by the fact that Christians may even be frightened of the possibility of encountering infinity and flee back into the safe comfort of explicitly formulated precepts.[31]

Rahner suggests two approaches to revitalize Christian spirituality and break it out of this imprisonment in concepts. First, he says, in the spirituality of the future there will be a certain necessary selectivity among the dogmas and doctrines. Second, he calls for the piety of the future to be a kind of mysticism which, although not forsaking the content of faith, focuses primarily and most essentially on the experience of trust in God which should ground all content.

In the past Rahner had been concerned about the discrepancy between the doctrines of the church and what Catholics actually believe. In the later writings he seems increasingly to accept the fact that this will be the normal situation for most Christians. In his article "The Spirituality of the Church of the Future," Rahner alleges that while culture in the past, not only in church but in society, encouraged a variety of devotions and interest in particular dogmas, today's secular and pluralistic world rather encourages a more intense focus on the essentials of Christian faith. In this world, "it may be presumed that far fewer individual flowers of Christian spirituality will be able to bloom."[32] Instead the focus of the spirituality of the future should be "that God is, that we can speak to him, that his ineffable incomprehensibility is itself the very heart of our existence and consequently our spirituality; that we can live and die with Jesus and properly with him alone in an ultimate freedom from all powers and authorities."[33]

God, grace, freedom, Jesus — these are what Rahner considers the essential foci for Christian life and meditation in the future. Although in the past he would have interpreted and retrieved the other dogmas in the light of these great dogmas, now he seems content to let the many doctrines rest (not denying them) while concentrating more intensely on the major ones. A good example of this approach is his work on short credal formulations for today.

The Ongoing Role of Short Credal Formulations

Rahner sees a real need now, as in the early church, for short formulas of faith which embody the essentials of belief in language comprehensible to men and women of different cultures and

experience. He advances four major reasons for the need for short
formulas of faith today. First, without such short easily
remembered formulas the faith that is learned in instruction easily
becomes vague and distorted. There is especially the danger of
elevating secondary matters to primary positions in the exercise
of one's religion. Short formulas keep constantly before one's
eyes the essentials of faith. Second, creeds can present a credible
account of faith to modern unbelievers which, through an element
of critique of actual Christians and Christian practice,
distinguishes Christianity from its distortions and misrepresen-
tations. Third, Christians no longer live in a world permeated
with Christianity. In the past one could presume that the essentials
of Christianity were understood by all so attention could be given
to secondary matters. In today's secular world attention must
be given to the essentials. And finally the need for new creeds
is advanced because the Apostles' Creed and the other ancient
creeds "cannot simply perform the function of a basic summary
of the faith today in an adequate way because. . .[they do]. . .not
appeal directly enough to our contemporary intellectual and
spiritual situation."[34]

The presumption that lies behind all these reasons for the
need of short formulas is Rahner's conviction of the continuing
need of formulations of faith. On the one hand, he certainly points
out the relativity of propositions. Faith must be "vulnerable. . .
continually breaking through the clear definitions of formulas
into the incomprehensibility of God."[35] On the other hand, faith
finds its fullness when it is expressed in concrete formulations.
Although he recognizes that in today's world the overwhelming
emphasis is on praxis rather than on theory, and that popular
opinion would perhaps focus more readily on Christian living
than on doctrinal schemes, he presupposes "that Christianity,
in contrast to other religions, cannot dispense with a certain
conceptualized statement of its beliefs as an element inherent in its

own nature."[36] But Rahner never absolutizes the word. He always sees a dynamism present between the word and the reality to which it refers.

These creeds point to the simplification and return to essentials which becomes an increasingly central motif in his later writing. Today's situation calls for a plurality of creeds suited to different people and different levels of understanding. These creeds must arise out of the experience of the people for whom they are written so that they will not appear foreign or extrinsic. For such creeds to be useful in today's church, Rahner says, they must be brief, "capable of being directly and existentially assimilated, self-explanatory. . . .They must be illuminating within the particular man's perspective of understanding and experience of life, as far as possible using his modern vocabulary and employing those presuppositions which are self-evident to modern man. . . . They must not presuppose as already given anything which is not immediately intelligible as 'given' and cannot be fundamentally experienced."[37]

These brief creeds focus on the essentials of Christian faith. "Not everything which is true must for this reason be equally significant."[38] Their primary purpose should be to provide a starting point or a way into Christian faith for contemporary people, Christians or not. This involves a certain selection among the truths of Christianity as to those which are essential and those which are secondary. For the right to make such a selection Rahner appeals to the Decree on Ecumenism (*Unitatis Redintegratio*) which clearly states: "In Catholic teaching there exists an order or 'hierarchy' of truths, since they vary in their relationship to the foundation of Christian faith."[39]

The one absolute content requirement which Rahner proposes as necessary is that in order "to constitute a confession of Christian faith it must express belief in the historical Jesus as Our Lord, the bringer of salvation in the absolute."[40] The contents of the three creeds which Rahner proposes as examples echo the preoccupation of his whole theological endeavor with the three great Christian mysteries of Trinity, grace and incarnation. By focusing from different approaches on these three great mysteries in his suggested creeds which he calls theological, sociological or anthropological, and futurological he tries to draw the believer into contact with the whole of Christian faith.[41]

If, even for Christians, faith is based fundamentally on the transcendental experience of God and allows a certain selectivity among the doctrines, a practical question arises. As it is put in *Our Christian Faith,* ''How much of what the Church says must we believe?''[42] This is an existential problem for many Catholics, particularly young people. ''The great concepts of the faith and a thousand and one statements of traditional Christian piety no longer fit into a modern man's or woman's picture of the world, they no longer have any 'life situation'. The Church's doctrinal statements fall into a void, say nothing, and so give the impression of being unusable and useless.''[43] They are often identified with a perceived authoritarianism on the part of Rome or with a mythological interpretation which is incredible to today's Catholics. Thus, while still professing to be Catholic, many Catholics of today do not identify with many traditional Catholic doctrines. What is to be done about this?

In contrast to the early Rahner, the answer offered here is not primarily to demythologize the doctrines or to try to explain their authentic nature and relationship to human experience. Rather his answer here is to advise Christians to center their spiritual lives around those truths most important in the hierarchy of truths. In contrast to an understanding which sees people as outside the church or as heretics if they deny even a minor point of church dogma, Rahner underlines the core of belief to which Christians must be committed, the basic truths which he refers to again and again and which form the outline of *Foundations* and

the content of his short creeds.[44] With regard to any other truths
of faith — and Rahner explicitly includes original sin, infallibility
and the immaculate conception — he says, "No one is banned
from finding out more about such matters. But when this is not
possible, or one fails, or a person simply ignores such matters,
he or she is still a good faithful Catholic."[45] In fact, as noted
above, he suggests that among the average Catholics of today
this process of selectivity is not the abnormal way but the normal
way to be Catholic. (Although Rahner takes this approach with
the "average" Catholic, he himself as a theologian and teacher
still feels a deeper responsibility to the many dogmas of the church
and their interpretation.)[46]

Rahner says that there is no need for one to feel obliged
to leave the church or to feel dishonest in staying if one has not
existentially appropriated the dogmatic content of the catechism,
not to mention Denzinger. "It is not the case that the only
Christian faithful to the Church is the one who keeps in his or
her head, in a more or less complete and organized form, all
the doctrines to be found in Denzinger!"[47] Is this not heresy,
though, a denial of the truths of faith? Rahner says not. He
counsels such Christians not actually to deny doctrines they do
not understand or find meaningful, but just to let them rest.[48]
It is also the case that while a person may express a doubt about
a particular dogma or proposition, this is most often an opinion
and does not constitute a firm denial of faith. "Only a really
firm denial, with the whole weight of the freedom which decides
on life and death, would destroy an individual believer's positive
relationship to the consciousness of the faith of the Church as
a whole."[49]

Although this tentative approach to the dogma may not be
formal heresy, does it constitute the absolute assent of faith
required for salvation and membership in the church? Rahner
affirms this on the basis that skepticism with regard to various

individual dogmas does not imply absolute disbelief. Absolute assent of faith is not grounded ultimately in the various dogmas but in the attitude of absolute trust which has been referred to so frequently above. "If. . .you affirm the ultimate basic substance of Christianity, the existence of God, a prayerful relationship to him, an ultimate trust in Jesus as the unsurpassable self-promise of God to you, if you practice also a religious life in the Church. . .then you need not hesitate to regard yourself as a Catholic."[50] To the objection that this approach blurs the distinction between Catholics and other Christians, Rahner replies that it does just that and that in fact whether the churches have wanted to admit it or not the blurring of this distinction has been the case for a long time.[51] Rahner also suggests that this looser relationship of the Catholic to the church's teaching calls for a more pastoral approach on the part of the church to its official teaching. It might "consider more closely what it is required to proclaim to the people of our time with spirit and fire as the alpha and omega, and what it could afford to say more casually and perhaps even less precisely."[52] Mystagogy, or helping people to enter into contemplation of the depth dimension of Christian faith as manifested in its central doctrines, is the key pastoral task for today.[53]

More important than the appropriation of a multiplicity of doctrines is gaining deeper insight and experiencing more significantly the mystery which underlies all the dogmas and to which they point. Today's pastoral effort should be directed to helping people to break out of the categorical chains in which they have been imprisoned and to discover the deeper dimension of religion which can only be falteringly and imperfectly reflected in the propositions of faith. To this end Rahner says that the spirituality of the future must be pre-eminently a mystical spirituality, a spirituality which focuses on the depth dimension so often neglected in everyday Catholicism.

Mysticism: The Spirituality of the Future. Rahner's mysticism takes cognizance of the immense plurality found in the church of today and focuses on the unifying element of the transcendental experience of God which grounds all religion. Mysticism is "a radical experience of faith which destroys the conceptual and the categorial insofar as these claim to be ultimate realities."[54] Religious enthusiasm is a current popular expression of the mystical impulse, a kind of mysticism of the masses.

> Through religious enthusiasm the objectification of religion is dislodged from its system. The experience of being taken out of oneself makes what is normal and organized in the institutional Church seem provisional and questionable, incommensurate with the meaning it is supposed to signify. A man is thrown back upon his own subjectivity, which no longer appears manageable to him in terms of conceptual expressions and propositional criteria....All this at least enables a person to experience in a clear and inescapable manner his own transcendence and inner reference to God, itself sustained by God's self-communication.[55]

Religious enthusiasm is one way of bringing to consciousness the transcendental experience of grace and freedom which is the ultimate possibility of all human life. In whatever way it is described, Rahner is convinced that the mystical dimension has to be the future focus of Christian life and spirituality. "The Christian of the future will be a mystic or he will not exist at all."[56] A religion perceived as grounded in propositions and dogmas is not enough to sustain today's Christians. Without an awareness of the depth dimension they will lose faith and fade away, as many have already done. It is clear certainly that a complete entering into the Christian mystery involves both the awareness of graced existence and its proper articulation, but according to Rahner if one of these elements were to be lacking (as it often is) it would be far better that it be the propositional aspect.

Without a consciousness of the mystery dimension to which it points, a focus on dogma can lead to a situation where "the pious Christian suffers in his daily life from the mediation of true religious reality through conceptual expressions and has the terrible sensation of remaining fixed in a purely human realm without any authentic experience of God himself at all."[57] Somehow the church must encourage a spirituality which allows Christians to break through the conceptual formulae to contemplation of the mystery itself. "When will we grasp this teaching on grace not only in propositional formulae but also in clear and inescapable experience?"[58]

Rahner describes enthusiasm as a particular kind of mysticism, still involving some categorical content. His comments on other types of mystical experience also shed light on his understanding of the relative importance of the rational content of faith. There is, he says, a kind of "pure mysticism." "By mysticism is meant here a transcendent experience through grace which is not categorial."[59] Such a "clear dose" of mystical experience is, however, a rare and sporadic occurrence.[60] "It must be said that the free acceptance of man's reference to God's immediacy, established by grace, *normally* [my italics] takes place, not in an isolated mystical interiority, but...is brought about by the encounter with an *a posteriori*.' "[61] This is the "normal" mysticism for Rahner, the mysticism of everyday life. Although Rahner uses the term mysticism in several different ways, a primary and constant concern is helping Christians to uncover the mystery dimension which lies at the heart of their everyday lives. An illustration of this in his own life comes from a newspaper interview. "I once asked him what his own greatest religious experience was, and he said, 'immersion in the incomprehensibility of God and the death of Christ.' I asked whether this had occurred in prayer and meditation. He replied quickly, 'No, in life, in the ordinary things.' ''[62] If Rahner calls all Christians to be mystics as the ideal, to enter into the transcendent experience of God in the course of their daily lives, he implies by this that the less focus there is on the categorical content of faith, as an end in itself, the closer one comes to the fullness of the experience of God. ''The whole institutional structure, although it can never disappear entirely in this life, is nevertheless in itself a sign which is destined to destroy itself and disappear at the appearance of God.''[63]

Although Rahner would recognize that for everyday Christian life contact with the essential propositions of faith is necessary, it seems far more important to him that this mystical dimension of faith be present and attended to by all Christians. In the post-Vatican II writings he is freer to concentrate on the mystical tendency which has never been absent from his works, a tendency which can be attributed in large part to the spirituality of St. Ignatius by which he was most profoundly influenced. Rahner says himself that "his own theological thinking sprang from the practice of the Ignatian Exercises."[64]

The Influence of Ignatian Spirituality

The *Spiritual Exercises* begin with the subjectivity of the human person. Their influence on Rahner's theological starting point is obvious. Although much has been made of the influence of contemporary philosophy on Rahner's adoption of this starting point, commentators are now recognizing that the Ignatian influence is probably the most fundamental. The foundational impulse of Rahner's enterprise then is clearly theological and religious rather than philosophical. With respect to the role of mysticism, Ignatius, as interpreted by Rahner, makes some startling statements such as: ''Mystical experiences provide the whole content of faith, the totality of our understanding of God and the world, even supposing the Scriptures were to be lost.''[65]

In the *Exercises* the church takes a somewhat secondary place. The focus is on the individual's free decision before God who is understood as ''the guarantee that such absolute freedom is available to every individual and that it can and should be offered and required of a person.''[66] The hope of Ignatius in the *Exercises* was to share his own experience of God and help others to that same experience. ''All I say is I knew God, nameless and unfathomable, silent and yet near, bestowing himself upon me in his Trinity. I knew God beyond all concrete imaginings.''[67]

According to Rahner, Ignatius was a man of the church, but in a very nuanced sense. He has Ignatius say, ''The story of my mystical path proves, that my love for this Church, unconditional as it is in one sense, was far from being the be-all and the end-all of my existence. . . but a secondary force which springs from a nearness to God and receives from it its boundaries and its own distinctive mark.''[68] This seems to describe very well Rahner's own attitude to the church. Devotion to the church and its institutional apparatus should never appear as the goal of one's Christian life. In fact, as was mentioned above, the Christian does not look to the church in the first and only instance for instruction. ''The Christian is also in direct contact with God and his inspiration. . .is not simply imparted through the ecclesiastical apparatus.''[69]

And in the light of this the Christian must take a critical attitude toward the church. It is interesting in this context that Rahner's own relationship to the church, like Ignatius' was complex. His sometimes acerbic criticism came from a deep love for the church and a conviction that, though secondary in the sense described above, the church is essential as witnessing to the fundamental communitarian nature of Christianity. Ironically, although chided by the right for being too critical, Rahner was often criticized by the left as too loyal to the church. His friend Johann Baptist Metz said aptly, "He has this church in his guts, and feels its failures like indigestion."[70]

Rahner, through Ignatius, chides the Jesuits of the past for their over-focus on the institutional aspects of the church. "Your mistake in this optimistic kind of anthropology from below was in letting a large number of your theologians transfer divine grace into another world of the consciousness, contrary to the fundamental conviction of my Exercises. It was their opinion that without real experience it was only possible to know this grace through external indoctrination by the Church."[71] If one can identify Rahner with Ignatius here, as it seems one can, then we can conclude by saying that in its deepest dimensions Rahner's theology and, therefore his spirituality is a "mystical individualism."[72] It could also be concluded that like Ignatius, Rahner's theology fundamentally grows out of his own experience of God which is primarily a mystical one.

The mystical tendency which underlies the whole of Rahner's theology does not negate the importance of the church and its doctrines for a full Christian life, but it certainly relativizes them. Only in a life which is in the first place lived in conscious awareness of one's relationship to the transcendent ground of one's being can the doctrines which represent the church's attempt to articulate that experience at various times have any meaning or saving significance. The centrality of this mysticism to Rahner's theology is clearly illustrated by its relationship to the Ignatian spirituality out of which it developed.

In his writings on spirituality and the lives of Christians today, then, Rahner breaks out of the positivistic emphasis on dogma so characteristic of the post-reformation church. He accepts a selectivity on the part of the average Christian toward the dogma of the church and indicates that people may consider themselves as belonging to the church even with widely varying degrees of relationship to its doctrines. He lists innumerable times what he regards as the essentials for belief — belief in God who reaches out to us, and in Jesus as the historical manifestation of that experience. Central to his theology at this later stage is the development in people of an awareness of their own grace-filled relationship with God in order that they may meaningfully appropriate to themselves in a deeper and deeper fashion the *essential* doctrines of faith.

For him the variety of dogmas *may* play a role in the lives of Christians but only the very central affirmations of faith *must* figure existentially in those called to explicit Christianity. And these also must be seen to be grounded in the fundamental transcendental experience of God which alone is absolutely necessary for salvation. Ultimately he sees all Christians as called to a mysticism without which the categorical content of faith is lifeless.

Notes

¹ "The Immaculate Conception," *TI* I: 213.

² "The Dogma of the Immaculate Conception in Our Spiritual Life," *TI* III, trans. Karl-H. and Boniface Kruger (Baltimore: Helicon Press, 1967), p. 129.

³ *Mary Mother of the Lord,* trans. W.J. O'Hara (Wheathampstead Hertfordshire: Anthony Clarke Books, 1963), p. 46.

⁴ "The Immaculate Conception in Our Spiritual Life," *TI* III: 136–137.

⁵ Examples of this approach may be found in the famous article on Christology, "Current Problems in Christology," *TI* I: 149-200; "The Interpretation of the Dogma of the Assumption," *TI* I: 215-227; in the more popular volume of essays entitled *Everyday Faith,* trans. W.J. O'Hara (New York: Herder and Herder, 1968); "The Resurrection of the Body," *TI* II: 203-216. Volumes III and VII of the *Investigations* also contain numerous articles illustrating this approach. A particularly good example is " 'He Descended into Hell'," *TI* VII, trans. David Bourke (New York: Seabury, 1971), pp. 145-150. In this article Rahner takes a seldom meditated on truth of faith and turns it into a meditation on death — both Jesus' death and our own — and on the interrelatedness of death and life.

⁶ "Remarks on the Theology of Indulgences," *TI* II: 175; "The Resurrection of the Body," *TI* II: 203-205; "Dogmatic Questions on Easter," *TI* IV: 122.

⁷ "Remarks on the Theology of Indulgences," *TI* II: 175.

⁸ Ibid., p. 176.

⁹ "The Resurrection of the Body," *TI* II: 203.

¹⁰ "Christian Living Formerly and Today," *TI* VII: 14.

¹¹ Ibid.

¹² Ibid.

[13] "Mary and the Christian Image of Women," *TI* XIX, trans. Edward Quinn (New York: Crossroad, 1983), p. 213.

[14] *Foundations,* p. 12.

[15] Ibid., p. 2.

[16] Ibid.

[17] "Observations on the Problem of the 'Anonymous Christian,' " *TI* XIV: 293.

[18] *Meditations on Freedom and the Spirit,* p. 23.

[19] Ibid., p. 20.

[20] "The Foundation of Belief," *TI* XVI: 19; "Anonymous and Explicit Faith," *TI* XVI: 58.

[21] "The Foundation of Belief," *TI* XVI: 18-20; "Anonymous and Explicit Faith," *TI* XVI: 58-59.

[22] "Religious Feeling Inside and Outside the Church," *TI* XVII: 228.

[23] Ibid., p. 230.

[24] Ibid., p. 240.

[25] Ibid., p. 232.

[26] "On the Situation of Faith," *TI* XX: 21.

[27] "Does the Church Offer any Ultimate Certainties?" *TI* XIV: 51-52; "Anonymous and Explicit Faith," *TI* XVI: 58.

[28] "Christian Living Formerly and Today," *TI* VII: 4.

[29] "Reflections on a New Task for Fundamental Theology," *TI* XVI: 164.

[30] "Religious Enthusiasm and the Experience of Grace," *TI* XVI: 44-45.

[31] *Everyday Faith,* pp. 60-61.

[32] "The Spirituality of the Church of the Future," *TI* XX: 147.

[33] Ibid., p. 148.

[34] *Foundations,* p. 449. See also "The Need for a 'Short Formula' of Christian Faith," *TI* IX, trans. Graham Harrison (New York: Seabury, 1972), pp. 117-118; "Reflections on the

Problems Involved in Devising a Short Formula of the Faith,''
TI XI: 230-231.

³⁵ ''The Second Vatican Council's Challenge to Theology,''
TI IX: 21.

³⁶ ''Problems Involved in Devising a Short Formula of the
Faith,'' *TI* XI: 232.

³⁷ ''The Need for a 'Short Formula' of Christian Faith,''
TI IX: 118.

³⁸ *Foundations,* p. 452.

³⁹ *The Documents of Vatican II,* ed. Walter M. Abbott (New
York: Guild Press, 1966), p. 354.

⁴⁰ ''Problems in Devising a Short Formula,'' *TI* XI: 237.

⁴¹ ''Need for a 'Short Formula' of Christian Faith,'' *TI* IX:
121-125. See also ''Pluralism in Theology,'' *TI* XI: 23; ''Problems
in Devising a Short Formula,'' *TI* XI: 237-244; *Foundations,* pp.
454-459.

⁴² Karl Rahner and Karl-Heinz Weger, *Our Christian Faith,*
trans. Francis McDonagh (New York: Crossroad, 1980), p. 124.

⁴³ Ibid., p. 125.

⁴⁴ See *Our Christian Faith,* p. 135.

⁴⁵ Ibid.

⁴⁶ ''Courage for an Ecclesial Christianity,'' *TI* XX: 10.

⁴⁷ *Our Christian Faith,* p. 134.

⁴⁸ See ''On the Situation of Faith,'' *TI* XX: 31. Rahner says
that heresy only obtains when a Christian contradicts a dogma
in an absolute way as an ultimate decision. To be heresy the denial
must also have a public dimension. He counsels against a too
facile imputation of heresy against anyone and calls for tolerance
on both sides. On the one hand, the church should not too quickly
accuse an individual of heresy, but, on the other, an individual
who finds himself or herself in conflict with the church should
also have a spirit of tolerance and humility. See also *Meditations
on Freedom and the Spirit,* pp. 97-109.

[49] *Our Christian Faith,* p. 136; see also *Meditations on Freedom and the Spirit,* p. 28.

[50] "On the Situation of Faith," *TI* XX: 31.

[51] "Is Church Union Dogmatically Possible?" *TI* XVII: 207-214. In this article Rahner suggests that with respect to the actual faith of Christians today there remain few significant dogmatic differences. "The major Christian Churches of today could unite, even institutionally; their sense of faith presents no insuperable obstacle" (p. 214).

[52] *Our Christian Faith,* p. 138.

[53] The concept of mystagogy, Rahner says, "gives access to much of my theology." Bacik, *Apologetics,* p. ix.

[54] "Religious Enthusiasm and the Experience of Grace," *TI* XVI: 47. For fuller discussions of the experience of mysticism, see "Mystical Experience and Mystical Theology," *TI* XVII: 90-99 and Rahner, "Mysticism," *ET:* 1010-1011.

[55] "Religious Enthusiasm and the Experience of Grace," *TI* XVI: 46.

[56] "The Spirituality of the Church of the Future," *TI* XX: 149.

[57] "Religious Enthusiasm and the Experience of Grace," *TI* XVI: 44-45.

[58] Ibid., p. 45.

[59] Ibid., p. 43.

[60] Ibid.

[61] "On the Situation of Faith," *TI* XX: 29.

[62] Bacik, *National Catholic Reporter,* (April 20, 1984).

[63] "Religious Enthusiasm and the Experience of Grace," *TI* XVI: 46.

[64] Foreword, *TI* XVI: x. See Egan, " 'The Devout Christian of the Future Will...Be a "Mystic." ' Mysticism and Karl Rahner's Theology," in *Theology and Discovery: Essays in Honor of*

Karl Rahner, S.J., ed. William J. Kelly (Milwaukee: Marquette Univ. Press, 1980), pp. 140-141; O'Donovan, ''Living into Mystery. Karl Rahner's Reflections at 75.'' *America* 140 (1979), 178.

65 ''Piety and Retreats,'' *TI* XVI: 140; see also Karl Rahner and Paul Imhof, *Ignatius of Loyola,* trans. Rosaleen Ockenden (New York: Collins, 1979), p. 12.

66 ''Piety and Retreats,'' *TI* XVI: 141-142.

67 *Ignatius of Loyola,* p. 11.

68 Ibid., p. 27.

69 Ibid.

70 Quoted in Herbert Vorgrimler, *Understanding Karl Rahner,* trans. John Bowden (New York: Crossroad, 1986), p. 37.

71 *Ignatius of Loyola,* p. 32.

72 Ibid., p. 37.

CHAPTER 5

Political Dimensions of Dogma

Chapter 4 focused on Rahner's attempt to show how dogma can have a living function in the lives of *individual* Christians. Today, however, the critique of dogma focuses, perhaps most intensely, not on dogma's impact on individuals but on its impact, or lack of impact, on the social and political dimensions of life. What do the church's dogmas have to do with today's pressing social issues? This critique suggests that dogma inhibits the exercise of Christian responsibility for the world, or at least does not call forth that responsibility. Many of Rahner's later writings show an awareness of this praxis critique. "A concrete mystagogy must," he says, "be at the same time 'mystical and political.' "[1]

A dominant characteristic of theology in the late twentieth century is its focus on the praxis dimension of religion. Perhaps in reaction to the personalist and existentialist theologies of the mid-twentieth century, with their intense focus on the individual, current theologies shift the emphasis clearly to the social and political. These theologies do not negate the importance of the individual but rather see the individual as he or she fits into his or her social matrix. They also emphasize that the individual is not merely responsible for his or her own destiny as the existentialist theologies would seem to imply, but that individuals are constitutively related to and responsible for both their world and other human beings.

Johann Baptist Metz and Matthew Lamb, in particular, apply this general concern of all the politically and socially motivated theologies specifically to the problem of dogma. If dogma is to survive it must be clear that it leads to action on behalf of one's fellow human beings. Its survival is gravely threatened in the opinions of theologians such as Metz and Lamb, not intrinsically, from the nature of dogma itself, as some of its critics have alleged, but because of the misuse, misunderstandings or non-use to which dogmas have been subjected in their history. Dogmas can and must be recovered and understood in their true significance, as transformative not only of individuals but of society itself.

Rahner's theology has been criticized by some for an insensitivity to the political and social dimensions of reality. From the perspective of these more praxis-oriented theologies important questions can be raised to Rahner. Is dogma not merely a means of understanding truth or explaining it, but also and more importantly a means of *doing* the truth? Is dogma more than disclosive of reality? Does it have possibilities for transformation of that reality? Are Christians not only bound to *believe* the church's dogma but also to *do* it? In the words of Matthew Lamb, are we anathema not merely for failing to give intellectual assent to the dogmas, but, insofar as dogmas are rightly understood, for our failure to live them? "Dogmas are expressive of a knowledge born of transformative religious love — a 'love that is not to be just words or mere talk, but something real and active,' a love 'only by which we can be certain that we belong to the realm of truth' (1 John 3:18 f.). Insofar as dogmas are such a knowledge and we fail to live by them, our experience will be anathema."[2]

The critiques of Metz and Lamb exemplify the contemporary praxis critique of dogma which form a backdrop for a consideration of Rahner's positions. Since this critique is developed from the perspective of praxis-oriented theology, it is first necessary to define such a theology. Political theology includes "all those theologies which acknowledge that human action, or praxis, is not only the goal but the foundation of theory."[3] It is not one particular theology alongside others, but is seen by these theologians as foundational to all theology.

To bring the praxis perspective into centrality involves a reconstruction of religion to which dogma, as epitomizing a theoretical-conceptual focus, can seem an obstacle.[4] Thus both Lamb and Metz deal at some length with the issue of dogma in a politically reconstructed religion. They are remarkably positive about its place and possibilities in such a religion, particularly in view of the fact that both suggest that narrative, or story-telling, is the type of discourse most appropriate to theology today.

Metz and Lamb propose to recover dogma for contemporary praxis-oriented theology by applying to it a hermeneutics of suspicion as well as a hermeneutics of recovery. Just as no theology is politically innocent, so neither is dogma. It can have political roots as well as consequences. In order for the dogmas to gain or regain their rightful role as powerful statements of Christian belief which lead to action they must be studied critically to determine their original social and political contexts. By doing this the real possibility of unconsciously legitimizing unjust social structures along with the dogma can be avoided.

According to theologians such as Metz and Lamb it has been all too easy to perpetuate unjust conditions through an uncritical appropriation of dogma. This, Lamb says, is an inherent danger in what he calls a mediational theology such as that of Rahner. Mediational theologies try to disclose relationships between contemporary experience and the traditional religious doctrines. This Lamb finds dangerous. "Merely disclosive models of truth are incomplete, for what is disclosed may well be the alienating falsehood of biased theories, techniques, and human conduct (praxis) sedimented in repressive social structures.''[5] A hermeneutics of suspicion means that dogmas must also be investigated for their negative and alienating aspects so that these can be brought to light and dealt with.

According to praxis theologians, however, dogmas also have positive aspects. If they are analyzed, it will be discovered that they not only are disclosive of reality but have been and can be transformative of it. ''Dogmas usually *look back* to the origins of Christianity or even earlier. . . . This orientation towards the past has a stabilizing function. Its concern with origins serves the cause of social consolidation. It has become conventional to note the *conservative* political force of dogmas. What can be overlooked is their role as a form of *liberating protest*.''[6] Gerald O'Collins points out, for example, that the Chalcedonian definition contained implications which went beyond its obvious discussion of persons and natures. Its assertion that Christ was of one substance with *all* of us could be seen to contain a protest against slavery. Likewise the dogma of the immaculate conception could be seen as a protest against the inferior status of women.[7] These social implications of the dogmas as liberating protest against oppression, however, are most often not seen until much later, if at all.

The primary problem of dogma in this context is not so much that they have not been assented to intellectually, but that they have not been seen as a summons to act out in Christian life the liberating protests against injustice which they do contain. Dogmas ''are in danger of congealing into static forms if their imperatives for transformation are not lived out in practice.''[8]

In Metz's and Lamb's approaches to political theology, then, dogma is far from unimportant. They call for a critical recovery of the dogmas by means of a hermeneutics of suspicion and recovery so that they can function in Christian life perhaps as they never have before. True orthodoxy requires orthopraxis.[9]

Witness to the Dangerous Memory

Metz describes the function he envisions for dogma in the context of his understanding of memory as one of the primary categories of Christian faith. He describes faith as "a dangerous and at the same time liberating memory that oppresses and questions the present. . . . It mobilizes tradition as a dangerous tradition and therefore as a liberating force. . . . Christian faith can and must. . . be seen. . . as a subversive memory."[10] The church and its creeds and dogmas are the public witness of that dangerous memory. "The Church is, moreover, to some extent the form of its [the memory's] public character. In this sense, the Church's teachings and confessions of faith should be understood as formulae in which this challenging memory is publicly spelt out."[11]

In this understanding, the faith traditions such as dogmas and creeds in which the dangerous memory is passed on are quite important to full Christian faith. Metz criticizes those theologians who easily accept the fact that many Christians have little or no understanding of the official faith of the church. He reacts strongly against those who fall back on the *fides implicita* (cf. Rahner above) of such people who may in fact practice a highly superstitious folk religion. This approach, he says, leads to an elitism in which the true faith is seen to be largely the property of priests and professional theologians. Metz's political theology calls for the return of the faith, including its dogmas, to the people. This, he says, can only be done when the church recognizes its responsibility to take part in the struggle to overcome suffering and oppression. "The Church must. . . resolutely accept the fundamental fact that there is a suffering that cannot be passed over in silence or transfigured by religion, but that has to be combated and transformed. This is not a commandment given by an alien political ideology, but the price of the people's orthodoxy, the price that has to be paid if the people themselves are to become the Church."[12]

Orthopraxis, then, for Metz, is not mere political activism but is in fact the price that must be paid for true orthodoxy. The church and its dogma are thus very important in Metz's political theology. Faith is dogmatic faith and that dogmatic faith must be made accessible to all through a critical and collective remembering. "Dogmatic or confessed faith is being bound to doctrinal statements which can and must be understood as formulae of mankind's memory that is subversive and dangerous and that has been repressed and misunderstood. The criterion of the genuine Christianity of that memory is the critical and liberating dangerous quality which can redeem man and with which it is able to introduce the remembered message to the present age, with the result that men are...astonished and frightened by it and overcome by its force."[13] Metz thus has great hopes for dogma in his politically reconstructed theology.

Dogma is useless and antithetical to Christian religion, however, when its function of preserving the dangerous memory is lost. "These dogmatic formulae and confessions of faith are dead, meaningless and empty — they are, in other words, unsuited to the task of saving Christian identity and tradition in the collective memory — when there is no sign of their danger — to society and the Church — in their remembered contents, when this dangerous quality is extinguished by the mechanisms of its institutional mediation and when the formulae have the exclusive function of preserving the religion that transmits them."[14] In other words uncritical remembering and mere repetition are not true orthodoxy.

Dogma and Narrative Theology

The preferred form of discourse in political theology is narrative or story. Dogma, however, seems to be radically antithetical to narrative as a form of discourse. Indeed dogmatic theology, conceived of as abstract conceptualization, is often opposed by its critics to a narrative approach such as one finds in biblical texts. Can dogmatic theology be reconciled with the more narrative theological style increasingly characteristic of the late twentieth century? Metz thinks it can. He sees abstract or argumentative formulae as elements in the wider context of the narrative of Christianity and as subordinate to that. Rational argument, he says, has a relative value, i.e., "to protect the narrative memory of salvation in a scientific world." "The verbal content of Christianity should therefore be seen primarily as a major narrative which contains argumentative structures and elements and produces such structures."[15] The narrative is not merely an illustration of the ideas contained in dogmas and other propositions. Doctrinal formulae serve as clarification of the narrative and not the reverse.

These issues raised by Metz and Lamb obviously invite dialogue with the transcendental theology of Karl Rahner. His relation to this praxis critique has been the subject of much theological discussion.

Rahner and the Praxis Critique

Both Metz and Lamb discuss Rahner concretely in relationship to the praxis critique. Lamb points out that in many respects Metz's political theology represents a dialectical retrieval of Rahner's transcendental theology. "He negatively criticizes the transcendental-idealist conceptuality Rahner employs in formulating his theological positions, but Metz affirms the intellectual and spiritual performance out of which Rahner theologizes.''[16] Toward Rahner's theology, then, as toward the dogmas of the church, Metz and Lamb would advocate both a hermeneutics of suspicion and a hermeneutics of recovery. Rahner and Metz shared the same critical concern about church and society, Lamb suggests, but the particular ecclesial, political and social contexts of their times called forth their differing theological responses. Rahner's theology then remains in a critical, dialectical relationship with political theology. It is also recognized as a foundational impulse toward Latin American liberation theology. As Jon Sobrino comments, ''Long before Latin American liberation theology was known in Europe, Rahner practiced it as a theologian of love for 'his' world.''[17]

Although Rahner is neither a political nor a liberation theologian, there are elements in his theology which point to the developments of these later theologies. There is also explicit in Rahner's work a developing sensitivity to the need for attention to the social and political dimensions of Christian life. This sensitivity, although more developed in Rahner's later works, is not entirely absent from his earlier writings. The development of his own thought toward an emphasis more on the unity of dogma, as well as the wider perspective which characterized his theology after Vatican II, provided an impetus toward more explicit attention to praxis as did his ongoing conversation with Johann Baptist Metz, his friend and former student, whose critique from the perspective of political theology was by Rahner's own admission the only critique of his theology that he took seriously.[18] It is important, therefore, to look briefly at those elements in Rahner's theology which at least implicitly point toward the political and liberation theologies.

Rahner's basic approach to dogma (and this does not undergo any significant change) is positive. His hermeneutics is a hermeneutics of recovery, with relatively little suspicion. He does not deal with possible distortions, or even untruths which could have resulted from political or other manipulation of the dogmas as do theologians such as Metz and Lamb. For him dogma once defined is true and remains true with all the qualifications which have been referred to in previous chapters. One significant early reference to the issues raised by those who advocate a hermeneutics of suspicion occurs when he notes that one must consider "whether a statement which in itself must be described as true cannot also be over-hasty, presumptuous, and offensive, whether it does not also betray an unkind tendency in sinful man to 'dogmatize.' "[19] Basically, however, Rahner has a rather linear view of history. There is no taking things back; once a dogma is defined it must always be dealt with in any further development of faith.

There is also no explicit discussion of the praxiological impact, in the sense of social and political dimensions, which the dogma should have had in the past or could have in the present. He does not draw the implications from the Chalcedonian definition or the Marian dogmas that O'Collins described, although he does realize, for example, that, "Christendom had at all times (perhaps occasionally not very discreetly) stamped its knowledge of women on to the image of Mary."[20] He recognizes that this historical view of women, concretized in Mary, has had an impact on the actual lives of women and their place in church and society. For this reason, he says that an appropriate contemporary image of Mary "can perhaps be produced authentically for today only by women, by women theologians."[21] In spite of this positive, disclosive approach to dogma, however, Rahner's theology may be looked to for the seeds which later developed into a more explicit attention to praxis on his part and perhaps more importantly on the part of those who draw their inspiration from his theology.

Leo O'Donovan points out a number of elements which indicate a deeply practical dimension intrinsic to Karl Rahner's theology. He first notes that although critics and followers alike have been quick to classify Rahner as a "transcendental" theologian, he does not neglect the historical dimension.[22] O'Donovan underlines the constant dialectic in Rahner's thought between the transcendental and the categorical. He points out that Rahner's emphasis on the transcendental, as well as perhaps reflecting Rahner's personal predilection, was also conditioned by the theological needs of the time when he developed his early theological positions.

O'Donovan suggests, as do Metz and Lamb, that to concentrate exclusively on the transcendental characteristics of Rahner's theology is to forget the actual content of that theology, as well as personal aspects of Rahner's life. The content both of Rahner's theology and of his life indicates an awareness of the importance of the historical moment. He never composed a systematic theology but addressed himself in somewhat random fashion to the pressing needs of the contemporary church. "I only attempt to clarify those individual questions that modern readers are interested in understanding better. I would say that I have always done theology with a view to kerygma, preaching, pastoral care."[23] His treatment of these topics was always action-oriented. He aimed to recover the dogmas of the church so that they could once again have an impact on the lives and activity of Christians. In his works concerning Vatican II and its impact he obviously has in mind concrete changes that need to be made in the life and activity of the church.

Rahner many times pointed out that he did not consider himself in any way to be a mere theoretician. For him a purely theoretical theology is a useless theology. "Theology is only of interest when it constitutes a process of reflection (although obviously of course critical reflection) upon the faith of a Church

which is actually using this faith as the basis of its activities."[24]
In an article in *America* in honor of his seventy-fifth birthday,
Rahner reiterates the ultimately pastoral intent of his theology.

> However abstract and schoolmasterly my theology may
> have been, it still has had in the end a pastoral, minis-
> terial inspiration. I mean, I have never or at least very
> seldom done theology for theology's sake . . . . Both
> from a personal, existential concern, but also from . . .
> an understanding of pastoral needs, I hope and I think
> that my theology was never really 'art for art's sake'
> in the way that was usual in scholarly theology, at least
> in dogmatic theology, before my time . . . this type of
> learned retrospective theology for its own sake was
> really always foreign to me.[25]

Commenting on the relationship of Rahner's life to his
theology, Metz describes Rahner's theology as a type of narrative
biography and thus as a precursor to the more recent and more
explicitly narrative theologies. Metz says that a "biographical
dogmatic theology" or "theological biography" can help bridge
the gap between dogma and religious experience and can respond
to the "indirect suggestion that dogmatic theology has in itself
hardly anything at all to do with Christian praxis and therefore
cannot have any deep effect on it or change it in any way."[26]
He defines biographical theology as follows: "Theology is
biographical when the mystical biography of religious experience
in the concealed presence of God is written into the doxography
of faith."[27] Surprisingly, Metz sees Rahner as the paradigm of
such a biographical theology. How is Rahner a paradigm for
such a theology? "His work is quite simply a theologically
substantial report about life in the light of contemporary
Christianity . . . . Rahner's canon is life itself — not life as selected

by the theological canon, but life as it imposes itself and often uncomfortable life.''[28] His theology ''is a biographical dogmatic account of the simple, one might even venture to say the average, Christian, the mystical biography of an undramatic life.''[29] Rahner refused from the beginning to be bound by the classical questions of the dogmatic system. Even the most ordinary every-day activities like sleep or leisure became theological questions for him.[30] His theology is fundamentally not merely an abstract reflection based on the inner coherence of a theological system, but a reflection which grows out of life and returns to life.

On many levels, therefore, Rahner was sensitive to the historic moment and the need to respond to that moment. His later move from focusing on the many individual dogmas to consideration of faith more as a whole was a response to what he considered a new historical situation. And he recognized that our rapidly changing world would continue to demand new and creative theological responses. ''Insofar as the critique by Metz is correct, every concrete mystagogy must obviously from the very beginning consider the societal situation in the Christian praxis to which it addresses itself. If this is not sufficiently done in my theory of mystagogy . . . then this theory must be filled out.''[31] Lamb suggests that this is precisely the intent of Metz's so-called negative critique, to realize the actual intent of Rahner's theology by grounding it in concrete practice. ''For Metz, Rahner's achievements must be complemented by critical collaboration with the natural and human sciences; they must be explicitly related to the concrete histories of suffering associated with the struggles for liberation and redemption.''[32] On the other hand, O'Donovan reminds us that a theology too exclusively focused on Christian historical experience has its own dangers. ''We cannot return to Christian historical experience . . . unless we have an interpretative sense with which to read history. For there are no facts, whether of oppression or of liberation, without the commitment which interprets them."[33] Lamb suggests that what is needed is a critical recovery of a transcendental orientation which in dialectical relationship with praxis could "undertake a socially critical reconstruction of church teachings."[34]

The Love of God and Love of Neighbor

Rahner deals explicitly with the theme of active engagement with and for others in his writings on love, love of God and love of neighbor, and his explanation of the relationship of that love to knowledge, or truth. In one of his earliest and most philosophical works, *Hearers of the Word*, Rahner demonstrates the essential unity of knowledge and love which is foundational to his theology. Knowledge is never for its own sake; it is only valuable when it issues in love. "Love is seen to be the light of knowledge. A knowledge of the finite that is not willling to understand itself in its ultimate essence as reaching its own fulfillment only in love turns into darkness."[35] In a quote which sounds as if it could have come from one of the political or liberation theologians, Rahner maintains, "Hence truth is first the truth which we *do*, the deed in which we firmly posit ourself for ourself and for others, the deed which waits to see how it will be received."[36] This quote comes in fact from Rahner's work on the Trinity, in many ways a highly speculative volume, but one which nevertheless reflects in a strong way the practical direction which grounds even the most speculative of Rahner's works. For Rahner, mere orthodoxy with respect to dogma would be severely lacking. The truth of the dogmas if correctly understood *is* transformative; it leads to love both of God and of others.

This relationship of love of God and love for others is dealt with in a programmatic essay entitled "Reflections on the Unity of the Love of Neighbour and the Love of God," first published in 1965.[37] It is impossible in such a short space to indicate completely the significance of the article and its deep rootedness in the overall intentionality of Rahner's theology. But a few points drawn from it will illustrate the action dimension or other-directedness that is basic to Rahner's dogmatic theology. In this article he states in the strongest possible terms that love of others is essential to Christian living. It is impossible to conceive of love of God without love of one's neighbor. "The love of neighbour is not merely the preparation, effect, fruit and touchstone of the love of God but is itself an act of this love of God itself."[38] And the reverse of this is also true — a true act of love of God is love of the world and the neighbor.[39] In fact this love of neighbor is *the* essential human act. It is only through active love of one's neighbor that one can know God. Human knowing takes place fully only in the going out of oneself to the other which is love. "The act of personal love for another human being is therefore the all-embracing basic act of man which gives meaning, direction and measure to everything else."[40] Love of God and love of our neighbor are so inextricably united that one cannot conceive of a love of God independently of a concrete love for one's neighbor.

   The works on love of neighbor also give some attention to the unpredictability of history, a concern of political theologians.[41]

   The love of neighbour is not something which everyone already knows reflexively in the depth of his being; rather, it is that which is sent to man only through the experienced and suffered wholeness of life and still remains even then, indeed especially then, a nameless mystery. It would be necessary to show by an empirical and descriptive phenomenology of love, responsibility, loyalty, venture, and of the unfinished and eternal quality inherent in love, what breadths and depths are implied by love of the Thou, how man really experiences in it who he is.[42]

This early foundational article on love of neighbor is still largely individualistic. Rahner is also quite concerned in this article not to evacuate the vertical dimension of Christianity, the relationship of God and the human being, by collapsing it into a purely horizontal love of neighbor on the historical level. This is a caution which he retains but seems less central in future articles. These early articles, however, do point toward the less individualistic praxis-oriented theologies which were to follow. Rahner himself seems to foresee this development. "At the dawn of such a new epoch, 'love of neighbour' might easily be the root-word which really moves people and the key-word for today."[43] Rahner's relating of love of God and neighbor offers a rationale for considering the love of neighbor as the primary perspective through which to approach Christian life. In this view love of neighbor contains in fact the whole of the Christian message.

Rahner's theology then, on many levels, and from the beginning, has a deeply practical orientation. Although this is not clearly articulated as a methodology, it is not difficult to see the elements that political and liberation theologians could build on and further develop, given the changing world and church situations of the later twentieth century.

Although not ever adopting the political program of Metz and others, and indeed remaining suspicious of it in some respects, Rahner himself developed toward a more explicit consciousness of the social and political implications of Christianity. Many of his later writings indicate this trend. It is interesting that Rahner's increasing emphasis on the political and social responsibility of Christians parallels the movement already seen in his theology toward a simplifying and unifying of the faith in the face of the complexity of today's world. It seems to be in the relativizing of the many dogmas that Rahner is able to articulate more clearly the praxis implications of the major content of Christian faith.

A good illustration of this simplifying and focusing is found in the brief creeds to which we have referred before. The "Brief Anthropological Creed" expresses clearly the interconnection of knowledge and love within the doctrine of grace which really sums up the whole of the content of Christianity for Rahner.

> A person really discovers his true self in a genuine act of self-realization only if he risks himself radically for another. If he does this, he grasps unthematically or explicitly what we mean by God as the horizon, the guarantor and the radical depths of this love, the God who in his existentiell and historical self-communication made himself the realm within which such love is · possible. This love is meant in both an interpersonal and a social sense, and in the radical unity of both of these elements it is the ground and essence of the church.[44]

Here praxis is not only essential but comes first. One discovers both self and God through active love of neighbor.

In the later writings Rahner indicates even more clearly that he does not intend this love of neighbor to be taken in a purely individualistic sense. Christians have a responsibility to the world also in a social and political sense.

> Love of neighbour cannot possibly be itself if it lends grace and dignity merely to the private relations of

individuals. Today it must also be practiced particularly (though not only) as the responsibility of every person and every Christian for the social domain as such. It must take the form of justice and peace because in the end justice cannot be sought by a compromise of merely rational calculation, but only by the occurrence often enough in society and history of the absurd miracle of selfless love.[45]

Rahner goes on in this context to talk about the critical commitment of the church in society and bases this obligation on what might well be called the "dangerous memory" of Jesus who sided not with the comfortable but with the poor and dispossessed of society. This theme of the social and political ramifications of Christian faith, seen as a whole, appears with increasing frequency in Rahner's later works where he discusses such specific issues as peace, revolution and the church's role in development, to mention only a few.[46]

There is then a deep practical dimension in Rahner which becomes more and more explicit in his writings. During the changing historical context of his long life, his interest in retrieving the dogmas of the church was no mere antiquarian or intellectual exercise. He attempted to reformulate and reunderstand the great dogmas of Christianity so that they could once again be expressive of that "dangerous memory" which calls human beings both to action and contemplation. In his later writings he does this by a simplification and a focus on the main elements of faith so that Christians might once again recognize in these great mysteries the imperatives to action and contemplation which they express. This clearly involves a certain relativization of the multiplicity of dogmas. Rahner saw our time as the historic moment for an emphasis on the return into mystery rather than on developing more complex ways of describing that mystery.

This tendency toward simplification enabled Rahner to explicitate more clearly the dialectic between action and contemplation which lies at the very heart of his theology. Ultimately, for Rahner, the great dogmas of Christianity should lead us out of ourselves through our activity on behalf of our neighbor to a mystical and contemplative union with God as the incomprehensible mystery which grounds all our activity. A mystical theology is therefore at the same time a practical theology. Metz calls for ''a praxis of faith in mystical and political imitation.''[47] Although Rahner is not a political or liberation theologian, and although his theology remains open to the critiques of these theologians, his insights remain a permanent, mutually critical contribution to his theological successors.

Notes

[1] Bacik, *Apologetics*, p. x.

[2] Matthew Lamb, *Solidarity with Victims* (New York: Crossroad, 1982), p. 112.

[3] Ibid., p. 103.

[4] Ibid., p. 100.

[5] Ibid., p. 110.

[6] Gerald O'Collins, *Has Dogma a Future?* (London: Darton, Longman & Todd, 1975), p. 66.

[7] Ibid.

[8] Lamb, p. 111.

[9] Ibid., p. 141.

[10] Johann Baptist Metz, *Faith in History and Society*, trans. David Smith (New York: Seabury, 1980), p. 90.

[11] Ibid.

[12] Ibid., p. 142.

[13] Ibid., p. 202.

[14] Ibid.

[15] Ibid., pp. 213 and 216.

[16] Lamb, p. 117.

[17] Jon Sobrino, "Karl Rahner and Liberation Theology," *Theology Digest* 32 (1985), 260.

[18] Bacik, *Apologetics*, p. ix.

[19] *Kerygma and Dogma*, pp. 87-88.

[20] "Mary and the Christian Image of Women," *TI* XIX: 212.

[21] Ibid, p. 217.

[22] Leo O'Donovan, "Orthopraxis and Theological Method in Karl Rahner," in *Catholic Theological Society of America Proceedings* 35 (1980), 47-65.

[23] *Karl Rahner in Dialogue*, ed. Paul Imhof and Hubert Biallowons, translation edited by Harvey Egan (New York: Crossroad, 1986), p. 256.

[24] "Reflections on Methodology in Theology," *TI* XI: 81.

[25] O'Donovan, "Living into Mystery," *America* 140 (1979), 178-179.

[26] Metz, p. 220.

[27] Ibid.

[28] Ibid., p. 224.

[28] Ibid., p. 226.

[30] See for example, collections such as *Everyday Faith, Opportunities for Faith*, trans. Edward Quinn (New York: Seabury, 1984) and *Belief Today*, trans. Ray and Rosaleen Ockenden (New York: Sheed and Ward, 1967).

[31] Bacik, *Apologetics*, p. x.

[32] Lamb, p. 126.

[33] O'Donovan, *CTSAP*, p. 51.

[34] Lamb, p. 117.

[35] Rahner, *Reader*, p. 40.

[36] *The Trinity*, trans. Joseph Donceel (London: Burns & Oates, 1970), p. 96.

[37] "Reflections on the Unity of the Love of Neighbour and the Love of God," *TI* VI: 231-249.

[38] Ibid., p. 236.

[39] *Ignatius of Loyola*, p. 18.

[40] "Unity of Love of Neighbour and of God," *TI* VI: 241.

[41] See the hedgehog-hare fable in *Faith in History and Society*, pp. 161-163.

[42] "Unity of Love of Neighbour and of God," *TI* VI: 242.

[43] Ibid., p. 249.

[44] *Foundations*, p. 456.

[45] *Our Christian Faith*, p. 176.

⁴⁶ See "Radical Faith in Ordinary Times," in *Opportunities for Faith*, pp. 7-10; "Peace as Mandate," in *Opportunities*, pp. 94-107; "Practical Theology and Social Work in the Church," and "The Peace of God and the Peace of the World," in *TI* X, trans. David Bourke (New York: Seabury, 1973), pp. 349-388; "The Church's Commission to Bring Salvation and the Humanization of the World" and "On the Theology of Revolution," in *TI* XIV: 295-330; "Theological Justification of the Church's Development Work," in *TI* XX: 65-73.

⁴⁷ Metz, p. 77.

CHAPTER 6

The Future of Dogma

Karl Rahner's theology has had an enormous influence on twentieth century Roman Catholic thought. His developing interpretation of the role of dogma in Christian life represents somewhat of a paradigm for the journey of Roman Catholic theology from the period preceding Vatican II through the council days to the present post-conciliar age. His work contributes to the contemporary discussion about the role of dogma in the religion of the future and provides a foundation for and a transition to the more praxiologically based theologies of the present.

Does Rahner see a future role for dogma? The answer is yes *and* no. Rahner says no to many of the elements traditionally associated with dogma. He is against any understanding of it as merely identified with its juridical elements. In his important works on the nature of dogmatic statements, a way is opened beyond the static and a-historical approach to dogma characteristic of much of theology particularly since the nineteenth century. Dogma is not an end but a beginning. While attesting to the permanent truth of a reality, it does so in human and time-bound words and concepts and within a particular historical and philosophical framework. All these elements may, and must, change if the truth of the reality is to continue to be faithfully articulated in a new historical and cultural situation. Uninterpreted dogma can appear incredible and mythological to today's Catholic.

Rahner says no to an understanding of the magisterium

of the church as presenting dogmas to the faithful for assent purely on the basis of its formal authority. The magisterium must explicitate the relationship of such formulations to the central mysteries of faith. People should believe because of the compellingness of the content of faith statements, not merely because of their juridically binding presentation.

Rahner says no to any understanding of propositions as divorced from the reality which they falteringly articulate. He points a way beyond a "deposit of faith" theology which saw the later dogmas as a logical unfolding of an original set of propositions revealed by God and otherwise inaccessible to humankind. In his metaphysics of knowledge, Rahner inextricably connects the propositional content of faith to an original experience of revelation, the experience of God's gracious self-revealing love. All propositions of faith grow out of contact with that original experience as well as out of contact with previous articulations. Faith is not ultimately grounded in obedience to propositions but in free and loving contact with that mystery to which all propositions of faith, however inadequately, refer.

Rahner can be said, then, to reject much of what has been traditionally associated with dogma. In the sense in which many people understand both the idea of dogma and many of the individual dogmas, they rightly find obstacles to faith. Much of Rahner's early work on dogma was devoted to the effort to clear away the misconceptions about dogma which have made it a pejorative term in Christian thought. By this method, he attempted to retrieve the many dogmas of Christian faith so that they could once again play an active role in Christian life. This was an important and necessary task.

However, the major development in Rahner's thought beginning with the Vatican II years and becoming more decided in his writings of the mid to late 1970s and early 1980s brought about a change in emphasis. In the later writings he develops a positive and compelling vision for the role of dogma in today's church and the church of tomorrow, the world-church, which occupies a central place in Rahner's later thought. In this sense he says yes to a future for dogma, but dogma quite differently understood. In fact, because of the past narrow associations of the term dogma, it can be misleading to apply it to faith formulations of the future as Rahner conceives them. It better describes his conception to say that he envisions a continuing and vital role for plural formulations of faith in the contemporary situation.

This vision of the future of faith formulations is also grounded in Rahner's metaphysics of knowledge. There must continue to be attempts at articulating the experience of God which lies unthematically at the heart of every human existence because that experience bears within itself the dynamism toward articulation. The unthematic strives toward the thematic. Therefore, the categorical expression of faith continues to be significant for Rahner. In his later writings, however, Rahner stresses more the second movement in the relationship of the propositional content of faith to its source. In these writings he emphasizes the function of propositions as leading back into mystery. He sees this focus as called for by the historical, cultural and social exigencies of the present. A number of practical consequences for the future role of faith formulations follow from this conviction. He sees an end to the ongoing development of dogma in ever increasing numbers of binding propositions. The task today, he says, is to develop a hermeneutics of dogma which makes the great and central dogmas of the past once again living forces in Christian life. These dogmas, i.e., Trinity, grace and incarnation, as well as the early creeds, should be retained as touchstones of unity in a church which will become increasingly pluralistic in the future.

In the world-church of the future we can and should expect no more universal and binding faith articulations. The needs of this church will be better met by provisional and diverse formulations reflecting the concrete situation of a particular place and time. Short creeds will be very important in enabling people to concentrate on the essentials of Christian faith. Pastorally speaking the church can no longer expect all its members to appropriate and find helpful all the many and variegated doctrines of the past. The mystagogical effort of the church today should rather be directed at helping Christians grasp and actually live the most essential elements of Christian faith in a unified way. Over and over in his later writings Rahner emphasizes what he considers these essentials: the gracious God and the fullness of God's revelation in Jesus Christ.

Rahner's focus on the transcendental aspects of Christianity could imply a radical relativization of the propositional content of faith. In spite of protestations to the contrary, is the categorical content of faith deeply significant in Rahner's thought? There is no doubt some ambiguity here. In relationship to the positivist theology to which he is reacting, he does relativize dogma. The mystical tendency which runs through his writings also implies a certain relativizing of propositions. The normal way of faith, however, involves contact with its categorical content. On the other hand, no one who did not consider the categorical content of faith as truly significant could have spent his whole life in explaining and interpreting that content.

I would suggest that in respect to dogma Rahner places so much emphasis on the transcendental dimension because that dimension is what has been lost in the past. A propositional faith which has forgotten its reference to the reality out of which it grows is empty, sterile and lifeless. It ultimately results in a religion of legalist obedience and fear. It is from imprisonment in this type of religion that Rahner tries to liberate people today.

To this end he does place much emphasis on recovering the depth dimension of religious existence. Formulations of faith are necessary and helpful but only insofar as their connection to the experience of that mystery which grounds religious life is recognized and thematized.

A final contemporary concern about Rahner's understanding of dogma involves whether he neglects the praxis or political dimension of faith formulations. Certainly on the individual level that is not true. Rahner's whole enterprise, in both its early and its later moments, has been devoted to the pastoral, practical task of allowing dogma once again to become a motivating force in the actual living out of Christian life.

His writings, however, are open to the critique of theologians such as J.B. Metz and Matthew Lamb who call for more attention to the transformative and political implications of the recovery of Christian dogma. This is an element which is not expressly thematized in Rahner's work. The seeds for such a development are there, however, in his recognition of the essential relationship of love of God and of neighbor. In his later writings he recognizes more explicitly the necessary political dimension of Christian faith. He writes of the implications of Christian faith for revolution, for peace and for bringing about a more just world. That these elements of his theology are not so fully developed in his own work is a recognition of the fact that Rahner was a man of his time responding to its philosophical currents and historical needs. A new age is approaching, in fact has already begun. New dimensions of Christian faith will have to be emphasized to respond to the needs of *this* time. Rahner's theology is open to this development. Both Metz and Lamb explicitly recognize their indebtedness to Rahner's theology in developing their political approaches. They see within his life and theology the thrust toward the political and social implications which they find called for in today's world. Rahner himself states that this emphasis is not antithetical to his thought but represents a legitimate development in response to a new historical situation.[1] Even in his early writings on love of God and neighbor, he suspected that the insight into this unity might provide the key word for the theology of the future. Rahner's fundamental insight is that faith propositions alone without reference to the transcendent reality out of which they grow and to which they return will be lifeless. Ultimately it is not the dogma which is transformative of individuals and society but contact with God as the transcendent dimension of all human life into which dogma should lead.

There will be a future for faith formulations, Rahner says, as long as they facilitate that unity of contemplation of the holy mystery and love of our neighbor which is the essence of the Christian life.

Note

[1] Bacik, *Apologetics*, pp. ix-x.